The Spy's Handbook

Herbie Brennan is a professional writer whose work has appeared in more than fifty countries. He began a career in journalism at the age of eighteen and when he was twenty-four became the youngest newspaper editor in his native Ireland.

By his mid-twenties, he had published his first novel, an historical romance brought out by Doubleday in New York. At age thirty, he made the decision to devote his time to full-length works of fiction for both adults and children. Since then he has published more than ninety books, many of them international best-sellers, for both adults and children.

Other books by Herbie Brennan
published by Faber & Faber

Space Quest
111 peculiar questions about the universe and beyond

The Spy's Handbook

Herbie Brennan

Illustrated by The Maltings

faber and faber

ILLUSTRATED BY THE MALTINGS

First published in 2003 by Faber and Faber Limited
3 Queen Square, London WC1N 3AU

Typeset by Faber and Faber Limited
Printed in England by Bookmarque Ltd

A CIP record for this book is available from the British Library

ISBN 0-571-21672 2

2 4 6 8 10 9 7 5 3 1

Contents

This one is for Jason, with thanks for the help!

So You Want To Be A Spy...?

A message from the author

So you want to creep around finding out what other people are up to? So you want to sneak into places where you shouldn't go? So you want to send secret messages, pass unseen through crowded streets, listen in to conversations, poke your nose into everything that's none of your damn business? **Fantastic!** This is just the book for you.

Spying is one of the world's oldest professions. Long before James Bond, Moses dispatched twelve field agents (Shammua, Shaphat, Caleb, Igal, Oshea, Palti, Gaddiel, Gaddi, Ammiel, Sethur, Nahbi and Geuel) to spy out the land of Canaan. They were briefed to bring him information on the people who lived there, the state of their fortifications and whether their land was worth taking from them. You can find out what happened by reading chapter 13 of the Book of Numbers in the Old Testament.

Spying is also one of the world's most dangerous professions. Mata Hari, the glamorous Dutch girl who spied for the Germans during World War One was shot by a French firing squad on October 15, 1917. Other spies have been assassinated, electrocuted, poisoned, gassed, decapitated, hanged or jailed for life.

But spying is interesting as well. A good spy can change the world and several already have. It wasn't a scientist who figured out the secrets of the H-bomb for the Russians – it was a spy who stole them from America. It wasn't logical arguments or direct threats that brought American troops in to help the Allies during World War One – it was a coded German telegram cracked by British spies.

You'll learn how to do stuff like that (although hopefully on a slightly smaller scale) by reading this book. You'll learn about codes and secret messages, about drops and disguises, about bugging and tailing and a whole lot more.

You'll also learn how they're spying on you.

So turn up your collar, put on your shades and pull down the brim of your hat. It's time to plunge into the fascinating world of espionage.

The Spy's Charter

Here is a reproduction of the International Spy's Charter, which lists the strict code of morality and decency under which all spies work.

You'll notice that apart from the heading, the document is completely blank.

Learning The Lingo

So you've read the details in the Spy's Charter now you need to learn the lingo. Spying has a language all of its own. Part of it is the sort of trade talk that grows up in any profession. But some of it is closer to a code used so nobody outside your spy ring knows what you're up to. Study the specialised terms below before you start this handbook, so you're equipped to know what's going on.

Alpha – Code for a male surveillance target.

Artichoke – When you artichoke a spy, you use hypnotism, brainwashing and/or drugs to find out where his loyalties really lie.

Assets – The agents' friends or supporters you have in place for a particular spying operation.

Bagman – The agent who carries the money to pay other agents and bribe people.

Black bag job – An illegal operation, like burglary, fraud, blackmail etc., carried out as part of a spying mission.

Blown – What you are when your identity (or the nature of your operation) is discovered.

Boxed – As a spy you're boxed when they make you take a lie-detector test.

Bravo – Code name for a vehicle used in surveillance work.

Bugging – The use of special devices, usually electronic, to eavesdrop on conversations.

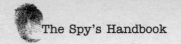

Burned – Caught in the act.

Charlie – A building, especially one under surveillance.

CIA – America's Central Intelligence Agency with headquarters in Langley, Virginia, which was founded in 1947.

Cipher – The method of creating a secret message by using symbols to represent the letters of the alphabet.

Cobbler – A member of a spy ring who forges documents and sometimes money.

Code – A method of creating a secret message by using symbols that represent words or phrases.

Code name – The name used to protect your identity when you become a spy, or to hide the real nature of one of your spying operations.

Control – An agent, or sometimes the spymaster, who directs the actions of a group of spies.

Courier – A member of a spy network who carries messages, usually without having the least idea what is in them.

Cover – A way of hiding your spying activities by pretending you're doing something else.

Cut-out – A go-between who makes sure there is never any direct contact between you and your control or spymaster.

Dead drop – Somewhere you can leave messages (or occasionally equipment) for other spies in your spy ring.

Disinformation – Pack of lies.

Double agent – A spy who works for two opposing sides at the same time, but is only really loyal to one of them.

Echo – A female surveillance target.

Eyeball – Surveillance operative in direct line of sight to the target.

Executive action – Murder sanctioned by the head of your spy ring. Executive action is NOT covered in this handbook.

FBI – America's Federal Bureau of Investigation, with headquarters in Washington, DC, has the job of finding foreign spies in the United States and countering their activities.

Foxtrot – Surveillance on foot.

Friends – How members of MI5 (and the British Diplomatic Service) refer to members of MI6.

Ghoul – A spy who collects the names of dead children from graveyards so they can be used as cover names for spies.

Going naked – Spying without a cover story.

Going swimming – Travelling.

Honey trap – A special type of set-up in which a spy deliberately provokes a romantic interest in a target subject in order to extract information or persuade the subject to work for the spy ring.

Intelligence – Secret information.

Legend – A false life story given to a spy to hide his real identity.

Live drop – A meeting place where you can pass messages etc. directly to other spies in your spy ring.

MI5 – Military Intelligence Dept. 5, the British Counterintelligence Agency, set up in 1909 to combat spying activities directed against Britain and widely believed to be the best in the world.

MI6 – Military Intelligence Dept. 6, the British Intelligence Agency which, according to official statements, does not actually exist, was never founded in 1911 and isn't funded by the British taxpayer to the tune of more than £70 million a year.

Mole – A spy who infiltrates an enemy spy ring to report on its activities.

Notional agent – A spy who doesn't really exist, usually dreamed up by a spymaster to mislead his enemies about something. (See Operation Mincemeat in the chapter on Astounding Cases).

Paroles – Special code words used by spies to identify each other.

Plumber – The spy responsible for any break-ins during an operation.

Raven – A male spy who specialises in romantic methods of extracting information from a target female.

Shadow – To follow somebody secretly. Can also mean the person doing the following.

Shoe – A fake passport.

Shopping list – The information your controller wants you to bring back during an operation.

Signposting – Secretly marking a drop to show your colleague this is the one that's in use; or alternatively signalling a particular course of action through the use of a secret sign.

Sleeper – An agent left innocently in place, sometimes for years, before being activated for a particular operation.

Spook – American slang term for a spy.

Spymaster – The agent in charge of a spy ring.

Stringer – A freelance spy.

Swallow – A female spy who specialises in romantic methods of extracting information from a target male.

Target – A person under observation during a surveillance mission.

Terminated with extreme prejudice – Murdered. (Something else not covered in this handbook.)

Triple agent – A double agent who's not really loyal to the side that thinks he is, but is actually working for the other side while pretending to the first side he is loyal to them and only pretending to work for the side he's secretly loyal to. Got that?

The Company – Insider term for the CIA in America.

The Cousins – What British spies call their counterparts in the CIA.

The Farm – CIA training school.

The jib – An inflatable dummy used by CIA spies to convince people they are still in place somewhere when they've actually left, as when they leap athletically from moving cars. (No, honestly.)

The take – Information gathered by spies.

Throwaway – A cover story that no longer stands up, which is then replaced by a second, equally fictitious, cover story.

Uncle – The headquarters of a spy ring.

V-man – A trusted informer.

Wet job – A spying operation involving bloodshed.

Wire tap – The bugging of a phone line.

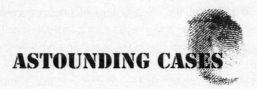

ASTOUNDING CASES

Since it's as well to know what you're getting into, here are a few examples of the sort of things spies get up to. You may find it hard to believe when you're reading them, but every case study quoted is absolutely true.

Operation Mincemeat

This one happened in 1943 while World War Two was in full swing and shows a spy can succeed in an operation even though he is dead before it starts.

Picture the scene. After a bad start, the war was going rather well for the Allies. They'd successfully invaded North Africa and were planning to do the same to Italy. But they wanted to make sure the Germans didn't know that. In fact, what they wanted was to convince the Germans they were going to invade Greece instead, thus diverting Nazi defences from the real target.

Enter British spymaster Ewen Montagu, who came up with a brilliant, if gruesome, scheme. He had the idea of co-opting a corpse into the British Intelligence Service and sending it on an undercover mission to fool the Germans.

Montagu eventually found a suitable body – a fit-looking 38-year-old man who had died from pneumonia. The cause of death was important because it left fluid in the lungs so it could easily seem the man had drowned at sea. After getting permission from the dead man's relatives, Montagu put his plan in motion. Like any other good spy, the corpse was given a new identity. It was issued with (false) papers in the name of William Martin, a Major in the Royal Marines and a Staff Officer in the Command Centre for Mediterranean operations.

As well as the phony ID, a watertight briefcase chained to the body's wrist contained a top secret coded letter written by a British general explaining how the Allies hoped to convince the Germans they were definitely not going to invade Greece when, in fact, they were. (This was a double bluff, of course: you have to remember the Allies were actually going to invade Italy.) Several other items – a photograph of 'Major Martin's' girlfriend, love letters, ticket stubs for a London theatre etc. – were included to give an authentic feel.

Then the body was dumped overboard from a submarine near the beach at Huelva in Spain.

The corpse was picked up by fishermen and turned over to the Spanish authorities, who were sympathetic towards the Nazis during the war. As Montagu hoped they might, they passed copies of the documents – including the coded letter – on to the Germans before returning body and briefcase to the British.

Nazi experts cracked the code and bought the story. The Germans promptly strengthened their defences in Greece and were caught completely unawares when the Allies struck in Italy. Operation Mincemeat, as the whole affair was code-named, proved a complete success… all because of a secret agent who was stone cold dead before it even started.

Pay-offs

While some spies work for love of their country and some for the sheer excitement of their job, many more go into the business purely for the money. But sometimes the pay-off isn't what they'd hoped.

Take the case of Cicero, for example, code name for the Albanian Elyeza Bazna, one of the most successful spies in history.

Cicero had no spying experience at all when he moved with his wife and children to Ankara, the capital of Turkey. But in 1943, he landed a job as personal valet to the British Ambassador and decided it was the perfect opportunity to go into the espionage business.

First of all, Cicero made a copy of the key to the Ambassador's personal dispatch box. Then he found the combination of the Residency safe. In just two moves, he had gained access to every secret British document in Turkey. His next move was to make some money out of it.

On the night of October 26, Cicero made contact with a German intelligence officer named L. C. Moyzisch and offered to bring him copies of Britain's most secret documents for a payment of £20,000.

It was a tempting offer. Britain and Germany were at war at the time, so any secret documents were particularly important. But £20,000 was a vast sum of money in those days and Cicero was demanding it in cash, pounds sterling. Even though he offered to drop the price to £15,000 for future deliveries, Moyzisch told him he would have to clear things with his superiors.

The following day, Moyzisch went to the German Ambassador in Turkey who sent a coded message to the German Foreign Minister in Berlin. Rather to their surprise, the Minister replied that Cicero's offer should be accepted and a courier was being dispatched immediately with the money.

Throughout the remainder of that year, Cicero provided Moyzisch with film after film of British documents, collecting huge pay-offs each time he did so.

Then, in spring of 1944, Cicero suddenly found his cover blown. A highly placed Allied spy in the German Foreign Ministry discovered there was secret information coming out of the British Embassy in Ankara.

At first, Embassy staff were not able to discover who the spy in their midst actually was, but then a German defector identified Bazna as the elusive Cicero. The Ambassador called him in and fired him, even though Bazna denied everything.

By this time, Cicero had £300,000 in British bank notes salted away, a sum worth many millions in today's currency. He booked a passage for South America, banked his loot and rented a villa overlooking the ocean. It seemed as if there could not have been a happier ending to his career in spying.

But then his South American bankers arrived at his villa with the news that almost all the bank notes he had deposited were forgeries. The Germans had been paying him in duff money.

Cicero ended up in prison, but even his collection of worthless bank notes was not the meanest pay-off ever given to a spy. The reward collected by Alexander Szek was much worse.

Szek was a young radio operator working for the Germans in occupied Belgium shortly after the start of World War One. He was recruited as a spy by British spymaster Reginald Hall, who discovered Szek had actually been born in Croydon. Hall sent word that if Szek didn't steal the German code book, his family in Britain would be arrested.

Szek agreed to do the best he could, but since he had no way to get his hands on the entire book, he decided to memorise the codes a few lines at a time, then write them down and have the copies smuggled to England.

The plan worked well enough, but Szek became more and more nervous about the possibility of discovery. So much so, in fact, that his cut-out reported he was on the verge of a nervous breakdown. When Szek pleaded to be smuggled out of Belgium, Hall finally agreed, but only after Szek had delivered the last page of the codes.

Szek crossed the border into Holland and handed the final codes to the British military attaché in The Hague. He was told to return to Brussels and wait there for the agents who would shortly smuggle him out to England. Szek did so and was dead in a week. The British authorities paid a hit man £1000 to kill him in case he made a break for it and thus alerted the Germans to the possibility he had stolen their codes.

World's Worst Spy

If Alexander Szek was one of history's unluckiest spies (the British obtained all the German codes from another source only months after they killed him), the world's worst seems to have been Michael Bettany. Bettany, who was born in Stoke-on-Trent, had huge problems deciding what he wanted to do with his life. He was attracted to Nazi doctrines, then changed his mind and became a Communist instead. He thought of entering the priesthood, but actually took up a teaching post in Germany. Eventually, in 1982, he became a spy for MI5, the British Counterintelligence Service.

Just what sort of secret agent he was going to be became obvious shortly afterwards when Bettany staggered drunkenly onto a train without a ticket, then ran when the conductor approached him. The conductor chased him down the corridor, but Bettany made such a fuss that the police had to be called. When they arrived, he shouted loudly, "You can't arrest me – I'm a spy!"

Although this was not the only time Bettany got himself into trouble, MI5 promptly promoted him to the Russian Desk, one of the most important posts in the entire organization. There he learned the names of all the KGB agents operating in Britain and decided to become a double agent himself.

To this end, he made copies of secret documents and stuffed them through the letter box of a Russian diplomat with a cover note explaining he was a member of MI5 who wanted to spy for the Soviets. When this didn't work, he called on several other Russian diplomats. None of them believed him for a minute. What real spy would act so stupidly or so openly? They decided eventually that the approaches were a bungling attempt by the British to plant Bettany in Russia as a double agent.

To put a stop to the nonsense, the KGB simply informed MI5 they had an officer who was trying to sell secrets – the Russian way of saying they were not about to be fooled. The Russians were astonished when Bettany was arrested. They simply could not believe this bumbling idiot was what he claimed to be.

Bettany, who told his MI5 colleagues that, "only the Soviet system can appreciate a man like me," was given a 23-year jail term although he had failed completely to sell a single British secret.

Setting up a spy ring is easy – it's setting up a good one that's hard.

SETTING UP A SPY RING

You can start with just a friend and yourself, although it's far more fun if there are three or four of you. But don't make it too big. Remember, the more people who know about an espionage operation, the more chances there are of somebody letting something slip. A good, manageable number is six.

Before you go any further, you have a few decisions to make. The most important is whether you want to be a field agent or a spymaster.

As a field agent, you get to work at the sharp end of the business, sneaking around in disguise, bugging people's houses, copying secret documents. But as a spymaster, you get to tell field agents what to do and all the secrets collected by the entire spy ring end up in your hands. What's more, if you set things up properly, there's far less chance of your getting caught than there is for a field agent.

Since you're going to set up the spy ring in the first place, you're going to have to take the job of spymaster, at least until things are going smoothly and you can pass it on to somebody else. But that doesn't mean you have to miss the fun of being a field agent – you can always do both. To start with, however, concentrate on being spymaster until your spy ring is in place. Now for setting up your spy ring…

Find Your Uncle

First find your uncle, the headquarters from which your spy ring will be run. This will be the place where you will store (preferably well hidden) all the intelligence information collected by your field agents. It's also the place where you'll keep code books, cipher machines, training manuals (this one at least) and equipment like false beards or exploding dentures for issue to your agents.

Your room at home might do at a pinch, although you need to be sure your ghastly little brother or sister won't poke around while you're not there. And you'll need to undertake your own cleaning – that'll please your mother – otherwise you run the risk of somebody stumbling on your secrets by accident. As an additional level of security, you can put in place some of the tricks and traps outlined later in this handbook.

Once you've set up your uncle, you can begin recruiting your field agents. Never do this directly. A spy ring where everybody knows everybody else is completely vulnerable the minute an agent's cover is blown. What you need to do is find yourself a control, a cut-out who stands between you and your field agents.

In Control

Obviously you're going to need somebody you can trust, but let's not make it your best friend. That would point the finger straight at you if anybody was trying to find the mastermind behind the ring.

How should you approach your control? The answer is... carefully. Don't rush in with the news you're trying to set up a spy ring. If the person you're approaching turns down your offer, you've blown everything for no reason at all.

What you need is subtlety, a little roundabout conversation, a cautious sounding-out about their interest in espionage, followed – if everything has gone well – by an offer they can't refuse.

There's one great secret of persuading people to do what you want them to do – put yourself in the other person's place. Try to see the situation from their point of view. This means that when you're setting up a spy network you don't ask for favours or start explaining how important the whole thing is to you. Instead, you stress the fun a spy ring would be for the other person and explain the benefits (s)he'll enjoy from running a group of spies.

Then, when you've got him really interested, tell him confidently you know of an amazing spy ring that needs a control and you might, just might, be able to get him the job. This is, of course, a lie so even before you've set up your organization, you're behaving exactly the way a good spy should, covering your tracks, sowing confusion and bending the truth to suit yourself.

At this point, one of two things can happen. Your potential control can either say yes or no.

If he says no, you're no worse off than you were to begin with. The person you've approached doesn't know you're trying to set up a spy ring, doesn't know you're actually the spymaster. If he believed your cover story, he thinks he knows there's already a spy ring at work somewhere, but has no idea who might be involved in it. All you have to do is leave him in this happy state of bewilderment and find yourself another control.

If he says yes, wait a week or ten days before approaching him again, then tell him your contact in the spy ring insists he has to recruit at least four field agents for the organization before he can join. Once he's done so, he's to leave a coded message in a dead drop* and return two days later for his instructions.

Where Nobody Knows Your Name

See what you've done here? With just a little lying and deceit, you've set up your own spy ring *and nobody but you knows for sure you're involved!* The control you've recruited is getting his instructions at a dead drop, so they could be coming from anybody. He doesn't know the name of his spymaster, nor do the field agents he's recruited. If you've told your cover story well, he may not suspect you're actually a member of the spy ring, but even if he does he won't know your position and can't prove a thing in any case.

Once your spy ring is in place, you can use it any way you want, but here's a neat idea. Why not set up two spy rings and have them

*We'll be dealing with coded messages and how to set up a dead drop later

spy on each other? Set up your second exactly the same way you set up your first, then quietly pass it on to a new spymaster ... without, however, mentioning your other spy ring. You have to leave yourself with some advantage when it's spy versus spy ... fair play just doesn't come into it.

SETTING UP A DEAD DROP

A dead drop is a place where spies leave messages and/or pieces of equipment for each other. A good dead drop can be the making of a spy ring. A poor one guarantees your cover will be blown in a month.

Take your time setting up your drop. Spend a few days, maybe even a few weeks, scouting out your neighbourhood for somewhere suitable.

Finding The Right Location

The first thing to remember is that it has to be in a public place. It's pointless having a dead drop on private property. Even if the owners are seldom around, Murphy's Law* dictates they're bound to turn up, with all their relatives, a brass band and the entire Territorial Army, the very second you're about to put something into (or take something out of) the drop. How are you going to explain the fact you're trespassing – or the bazooka you're carrying cunningly engineered to look like a plate of egg and chips? Your cover's blown. You're dead in the water.

But if a drop has to be in a public place, it can't be too public. You don't want to be spotted using it. So the ideal area to scout out is a park or library or even a large shopping centre or train station. Places like these have people coming and going all the time, so no-one will think twice if they see you there. But most of them have quiet

*Murphy's Law states: anything that can go wrong, will go wrong

corners where you should be able to establish a drop.

Let's look at some possibilities in each of them, starting with the public park since you probably need a bit of fresh air.

Park Possibilities

First, take all the time you need to observe the way people use the park. (This is something you'll have to do in *any* area you're scouting.) You'll find there are busy times, not-so-busy times and times when the place is almost deserted. Make a note of these times and also of any activities – road sweeping, park concerts, large inflows of rowdy schoolchildren etc. – that tend to take place at the same time each day. Activities like these can act as a diversion when you're using your drop.

In a park, the drop itself could be a hollow in a tree, a public wastebasket (but make sure your message isn't emptied with the rubbish), the underside of a bush, a loose brick at the base of a statue, a hole in a wall or any one of a dozen other hiding places you'll spot if you keep your eyes open.

But not all possible hiding places are good hiding places. When you find one that takes your fancy, ask yourself these questions:

 Is it overlooked? If there's a house or other building nearby someone could be watching every time you leave a message.

 Is it in too busy a spot? If there are people crowded around almost every minute of the day, you'll have no chance to use your drop.

 Is it in a suspicious area? If your drop is at the end of a lane that leads nowhere, it's only a matter of time before people start to wonder what on earth you're doing up there.

 Do you have a clear view in all directions? You need to be sure nobody is approaching when you use a drop. But remember, if you can see clearly in all directions, you can in turn be seen from all directions.

Is the drop sheltered or hidden in any way? If you're using a hole in a tree trunk, for example, the tree itself can hide what you're doing. So can a convenient bush or other feature.

 Is there a good cover reason for you to stop nearby? Nobody will think twice if you're looking at a statue, resting on a park bench or feeding the ducks on the pond. Features like these are useful cover for a drop and ensure people don't start to wonder why you keep hanging around the same spot. They also provide a convenient way to watch unobserved while you're waiting for somebody to leave a message at the drop for you.

Once you've established your drop, test it by approaching it from every possible direction. This will give you a very clear idea of how likely you are to be seen while using it and the direction from which an enemy might appear.

Finally, if at all possible, try to set up more than one drop. That way you can lower your risks by moving from one to the other at random and an enemy who spots one won't necessarily find them all – or be able to watch them all if he does.

What's been said about park drops applies broadly to other areas. Shopping centres and train stations tend to have very clear activity patterns which can vary with the day of the week. Once you know what they are, you can schedule your spy drop activities for the times when there are fewest people about.

Possible hiding places are, of course, very different to those you might find in a park, although some shopping malls and train stations do feature potted plants and bushes. But they also feature advertising displays, statuary and far more waste bins and public seats than you're likely to find in a park. As before, the place you select needs to be somewhere quiet so you can use it without attracting attention, but not so hidden that somebody can sneak up on you.

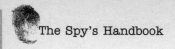

Public Libraries

Public libraries are particularly good places for a dead drop providing you only want to leave messages. The great thing about libraries is that they're full of books, you're encouraged to visit them and people actually expect you to hang about doing nothing in particular. (It's called browsing.) All this makes a library God's gift to a spy.

First, set up your cover by taking out a membership so you can use the library legally. As before, it can be useful to know when things are quiet, but this isn't nearly so critical in a library as it is in the places we've just been discussing: you can leave or pick up a message here quite safely even if you're jammed shoulder to shoulder with other users. The way you do it is this.

Take an hour or two browsing for unpopular books. Common sense will tell you not to waste your time on the latest Harry Potter – it's likely to be in and out like a piston. What you want are titles like *Teach Yourself Serbo-Croat, The Use of the Rivet in Victorian England* or *How to Exercise your Pet Piranha*. Check inside the front cover where the librarian's stamp will confirm just how often – or how seldom – a particular volume is borrowed. With patience you'll find a few that have never gone out at all. Obscure reference books are a particularly good category.

Make a note of the titles and the sections in which you found them. When you want to pass a message, code it – there's advice on that sort of thing later in the handbook – and slip it between the pages of a book on your list. Now all you have to do is let the recipient know the name of the book and the message can be collected at leisure. If you're worried that

an innocent reader may borrow the book, against all odds, before the message is collected, simply leave a duplicate in one of the other books on your list. Since you've picked really unpopular volumes, the chances against two being taken out at the same time are astronomical. And since your message was securely coded, it won't matter that a stranger has picked it up.

DISGUISING YOUR MESSAGE

If you're using a library as a drop, the most obvious way to disguise your message is to make it look like a bookmark. (Later sections of this handbook will show you how to create secret messages that give the innocent appearance of being something else entirely.)

Other possibilities are a page from a letter, a newspaper cutting, an old cinema ticket, a grocery bill... as any librarian will tell you, the things people leave between the pages of a book are legion.

You'll need to use a different approach when you're using a drop in the park or a shopping mall, but the principle remains the same – your message should look like something people would normally expect to find at the place in question.

Outside, for example, you might transform your message into a leaf or a twig. You can hollow out a piece of cane or stick easily enough using a screwdriver. Cut it to a convenient length, roll your message tightly and stuff it inside. If you take a large leaf and roll it around a pencil, you're on your way to making a message container that'll pass muster anywhere outdoors. Tie the leaf in place using string or an elastic band, then leave it to dry out. Once it has, you can slip it carefully off the pencil, remove the string and you have a wholly natural looking tube for your next message.

Hollow twigs can be recycled, but dried leaves are fragile and seldom last beyond a single usage, so you might think of making a batch of leaf tubes and storing them in your Spy Kit* for use as needed.

> One spy operating in central Europe hit on the idea of disguising his messages by hiding them in the corpses of hollowed-out rats. It worked wonderfully well for a time – nobody except another spy is keen to handle a dead rat. But then a cat ate his container, message and all, so he abandoned the method.
>
> All the same, the dead rat dead drop may encourage you to use your imagination. Pay a call to your nearest joke and novelty shop where you may find hideously realistic-looking items – such as artificial dog poo – that you can modify to hide messages.

Just Rubbish

In places like a shopping centre or train station, quite a good bet is to make your message look like litter. An empty soft drinks can will hide a message perfectly – so much so the recipient will usually have to cut the can to get it out. (But that's easy since most soft drink cans are made from very light aluminium.) Alternatively you can surround it in a crumpled candy bar wrapper.

The only real problem with messages looking like litter is that they are sometimes treated as litter and swept away. To avoid this, you can use the old under-the-bench trick. Put your message inside a small container – a matchbox is ideal – and stick it on the underside of a

*See the final section of this handbook

seat using a piece of well-chewed gum or double-sided tape if you're feeling fancy.

Since there are lots of public seats in shopping centres and train stations, you'll probably be spoiled for choice, but your drop doesn't actually have to be a seat. You can use the sticky matchbox under, or behind, advertising displays, ornaments, potted plants or anything else suitable.

SIGNPOSTING

If you're running several drops there may come a time when you can't manage to get word to your contact as to which one you plan to use. Even if you're only using one, it's useful to have some way of showing your contact when it's active. Both these problems are solved by signposting.

Signposting is the setting up of one or more signals to direct a spy to a particular drop and let him/her know there's something waiting to be collected.

Almost anything can be used as a signpost. Many spies favour the simple approach and make discreet chalk marks on poles or benches along the route to the drop. Others prefer elaborately coded signs which are special messages in themselves. A piece of string used as a signpost can be knotted in a variety of ways to tell a spy what's going on:

pick up message at drop as planned

danger: the drop is off

change of plan, come back tomorrow

 your cover is blown, leave the country immediately

 I have been captured by an enemy agent and forced to keep tying knots in this string

If you plan to use bits of string as a signpost, you should work out your own signal system rather than using the one above. That way, even somebody who's read this handbook will have no idea what your knots mean.

An alternative to knots in string might be marks on stones. Don't paint them on – that would be too obvious. A few scratches will only be noticed by someone actually looking for them and can tell the sort of simple story you need. The dots and dashes of Morse Code might be used to spell out a word or two, but here again it's really better to work up a simple code of your own.

It's also possible to create quite a complex series of messages using nothing more than a single leaf. Here are some possibilities:

A broken stalk	go to drop one
A stalk broken in two places	abort the mission
A stalk bent to pierce the front of the leaf	await instructions
A stalk bent to pierce the back of the leaf	return tomorrow
Leaf wrapped round a twig	your cover is blown
Leaf pierced by a twig	rob the Bank of England and head for South America

As always, these are purely suggestions to give you an idea how a leaf signpost might be used. You should decide your own meanings and, indeed, create different leaf signs of your own.

The leaf, string or other signal should be left in a pre-arranged spot to flag what's happening at the actual drop. The spy headed for the drop will normally remove the signpost to indicate she's been alerted by the signal. In a sophisticated operation, the signpost can even be replaced by a reply in similarly disguised form.

SETTING UP A LIVE DROP

There are, of course, times when a spy can't use – or possibly can't trust – a dead drop. Circumstances may call for contact face to face, for the certainty of knowing a message has been successfully passed and received. At such times, the spy makes what's called a live drop.

The details of a live drop are often prearranged. A contact will undertake to be at a certain spot at a certain time. As often as not, that's where it ends. But from time to time, a spy will meet the contact and a message will be passed. In other instances, the meeting will be set up specially.

Brief Encounters

Unlike a dead drop, the rendezvous spot does not have to be sheltered or remote. Indeed, many professional spies prefer somewhere really busy, with lots of distractions. You'll understand why in a moment.

Areas suitable for live drops include art galleries, museums, almost anywhere with a notice board, the park, a popular café, the local supermarket, a barber shop or hairdresser's, a school corridor or even just a busy street. All that's really needed is a place where two people might meet briefly, as if by accident.

Passing The Message

There are several ways of passing a message at a live drop. One of the simplest is the 'brush pass' in which one spy slips the message into another's hand as they walk past one another in the street. Done well it's almost undetectable.

A variation on the brush pass involves your bumping into your contact and slipping the message into his or her pocket. Done smoothly, this method – a sort of pickpocket move in reverse – is also almost undetectable, partly because of its speed, partly because the two bodies involved tend to hide what's going on from prying eyes. But simple though it is, it does require practice. It's a very good idea to hone your skills on this and the brush pass with the help of a friend before trying it for real.

Another simple method that works well in certain circumstances is what's called the 'lover's touch'. Visualise this scene. A boy and girl sit opposite one another in a crowded café, gazing into one another's eyes. The girl has her hand on the table. In a moment of high passion, the boy reaches over and places his hand on top of hers. Shocked by his presumption, the girl snatches her hand away. Disappointed, the boy withdraws his own hand.

Well, it's a bit Victorian, but it could still happen, although these days the girl would probably leave her hand in place for half an hour before snatching it away. But it still works as a live drop. When the girl placed her hand on the table, she had a message concealed beneath the palm. The boy places his hand on top in a loving gesture, the real purpose of which is to keep the message safely hidden when the girl takes her hand away. Once the girl does so, the boy simply slides the message back under his hand, palms it like a conjurer and drops it into his pocket.

An even simpler pass is the shared sweet trick. Here one of the two spies carries a bag of boiled sweets with him. Being a polite soul, he offers one to his companion ... who extracts the secret message from the bag along with the sweet.

This sort of thing works well if the two spies involved are supposed to know each other. If they're trying to appear strangers, other methods have to be brought into play. One is the borrowed map trick. In its original form, this message pass works best outside a tourist office. One spy emerges, carrying a map. The other, looking like a lost tourist, asks to borrow it, studies the map for a moment, then hands it back with thanks. It takes moments at most and looks like the most natural thing in the world, but the spy who borrowed the map now has the message that was hidden inside. Alternatively, of course, the borrower spy could hide a message in the map and pass it back.

You can easily dream up variations on the borrowed map pass that don't rely on a tourist cover. A spy with hay fever might borrow a handkerchief. A spy in a restaurant might borrow a menu.

Another favourite of the professional spy is the old newspaper ploy, a method that has the added benefit of involving no conversation or contact whatsoever between the two spies involved. Here again there can be imaginative variations on the theme, but in its basic version the newspaper ploy goes like this – an old lady sits on a park bench, enjoying the sunshine and eyeing up the talent. A neatly dressed businessman strolls up with a folded newspaper underneath his arm and sits down at the far end of the bench not too close to the old lady. He opens his newspaper and begins to read.

After a while, the businessman gets up and walks off, leaving his newspaper behind. The old lady glances at the headline (*Schoolteachers Assassinated*) picks up the paper and begins to read it. When she leaves, she takes it with her … and the secret message concealed inside.

Sometimes a borrowed item produces unexpected results, as illustrated by the following scenario – boy meets girl in art gallery. They don't appear to know one another, but they're standing side by side admiring a painting of *The Assassinated Schoolteacher* by Van Gogh.* There is information about the painting on a small plaque underneath. The boy leans forward to read it. He seems to be a keen art student, because he takes a pad from his pocket to make notes.

*That's Albert Van Gogh, of course – no relation to Vincent

But what's this – he can't find a pen? He turns to the girl and asks politely if he might borrow hers. The girl smiles, nods and hands him her pen. The boy makes his notes before handing it back.

By now you'll have realized a message pass is in progress. But who gets the message? If you thought it was the boy, you'd be wrong. The secret message actually went to the girl. The pen she handed him contained nothing – it was a perfectly ordinary pen. But the pen the boy handed back wasn't the same pen he received. He'd quietly exchanged it for an identical pen with a secret message inside.

The Switch

The business with the pen introduces us to one of the most popular ways of passing secret messages at a live drop – the switch. Spies absolutely love the switch and work hard to dream up different variations on the basic theme.

You've seen the basic theme in a multitude of spy movies. Two spies stand close to one another at a busy airport. Both carry identical briefcases. A beautiful woman approaches one of them and demands a light for her cigarette. The man sets down his briefcase to oblige her. The second spy turns to leave and in a lightning-fast move, exchanges his briefcase for the one on the ground. The switch has been made, the message/microfilm/gun/miniature H-bomb or whatever else was in the case, has been successfully passed on.

There are many variations, each one tailored to the area where the switch takes place. In a busy supermarket, for example, spies will often use the 'brown-bag switch'. Although supermarket bags aren't literally brown (at least not always) one bag of shopping looks much like any other. Two spies approach, chat briefly, then walk off with each other's shopping and the switch is made.

The hat switch, or sometimes the coat switch, is best suited to restaurants, beauty parlours, barber's shops and similar establishments. Hang up your hat or coat as you come in, take your colleague's hat or coat as you go out and read the secret messages left for you at leisure.

Finally, a switch you can use almost anywhere – the paperback book switch. Each spy is equipped with a well-thumbed copy of the same paperback. One 'accidentally' drops the book, the other picks it up for him ... but actually hands him the other copy, with a message inside.

INVISIBLE INK

Spies like codes and ciphers, but while you'll get plenty of information about both later in this handbook, the very best way to create a secret message is to convince people what they're holding isn't a message at all – or, if it is, it's an entirely innocent message.

One way of doing that is to employ invisible ink.

Although once used quite widely, invisible ink long ago went out of fashion in the professional espionage community. It was too obvious, the first thing people looked for and consequently not worth using. But it's been out of fashion for so long now that people have stopped checking for it. This means you can put it to good use from time to time, particularly in emergency situations.

Although there are a great many sophisticated invisible inks which only become visible when the paper is washed in a particular chemical, they are difficult to buy and impossible to make for yourself without specialist supplies and expert help. This is clearly a limitation on their usefulness. Your ideal invisible ink is one you can make quickly and easily, under any circumstances, without being detected, without special equipment or materials, even if your enemies have locked you up and thrown away the key.

The Toilet Solution

Sounds like a tall order, but such an ink exists, known only to the very best spies. Gross though it may seem, what we're talking about here is pee.

Depending on your fluid intake, it's likely you pee several times a day, even when you don't need invisible ink. It's also likely you do it in private, an ideal situation for a spy. Next time you go, take a little bottle with you and collect a sample. Stopper it well and don't leave it near your parents' drinks cabinet. You've just manufactured your personal supply of invisible ink.

You can test how well it works by using a nibbed pen or fine paintbrush to write a trial message – 'BUY ALL HERBIE BRENNAN'S BOOKS' is quite a good one – on a blank sheet of paper. It will be visible enough as you write, showing up very faintly green, but when the message dries, it will disappear completely. (If it doesn't, you should see a doctor.)

To make the message visible again, heat the paper. Waving it vaguely in front of a candle flame won't do the trick and is dangerous in any case, but a few moments in an oven will bring it up a treat. As the paper bakes, the wording comes up strongly in brown.

In The Kitchen

If you're the sort of wuss who just can't bear the thought of writing with pee, several fruit juices are just as effective. Experiment with the ones you find about the house, but you can take my word for it that lemon juice works well and the juice of a lemon mixed with the juice of an onion works even better. You can also use milk or vinegar or manufacture your own special ink by mixing a cup of sugar with a cup of water. (A cup of salt mixed with water works too.) You can even write an invisible message by sticking a matchstick into a juicy apple.

In all these cases, the message becomes visible when the paper is heated, but if you figure your enemies might know about heating paper, there's another method you might try which keeps the secret however much heat is applied. It's a bit tricky and messy, but worth the effort.

Making An Impression

To create your message, you'll need two sheets of plain white blank paper. Wet one thoroughly and lay it on a flat surface. Place the second, dry, sheet on top and write your message pressing down hard with a ball-point or pencil. When you've finished, take off the top sheet and destroy it. If you hold the (wet) bottom sheet up to a strong light, you'll be able to see your message, but as the paper dries out, it will disappear.

Heating paper prepared in this way won't bring the message back, but if you paint over the page using a weak watercolour or very watery ink, up it will come.

A variation on this method that uses no water is to 'write' your message, pressing down as hard as possible, with a ball-point that's run out of ink. The faint indentations won't be noticeable, but if you rub a coloured pencil evenly over the paper, the message will come up again.

You can get much the same effect by using a white crayon, or candle wax, to write the message on white paper, then brush over it with well-watered poster paint. Alternatively, you can try sprinkling the message with chalk dust or instant coffee powder.

Waterproof Writing

A really neat trick is to write your message using a waterproof marker. (It'll normally tell you on the package if a marker is waterproof.) When you've finished, paint the whole page black using watercolour or some other water-based paint. You'll end up with a picture you can entitle *Midnight in a Coal Mine*, but if a fellow spy holds it under a tap, your secret message will reappear.

Don't Be Obvious

So far I've described your invisible messages as if they were usually written on a blank sheet of paper, but that was only for the sake of clarity. There's nothing more suspicious than passing a blank sheet of paper to a fellow spy. If anybody intercepts it, they'll suspect a secret message at once.

The trick is to pass along something that looks innocent, or is specially designed to throw your enemy off the scent. You might, for example, pass on a little love note. (That's maybe not *entirely* innocent, but you know what I mean.) Anybody who intercepts it will be so fascinated by the content they'll never think of looking for the invisible message written between the lines or in the margins.

Even better is to create a heavily coded message which details plans for your next major espionage operation to be carried out secretly in Blackpool. If your message is intercepted, your enemy will crack the code eventually and head for Blackpool.* The real message (about your next major espionage operation in Huddersfield) is written invisibly in the spaces – and may itself be coded as well.

But your message doesn't have to look like a message at all. You can write invisibly on pictures, maps, theatre programmes or even, if you keep it short, the ticket to a greyhound race. And as you'll see in the next section, there are ways of passing secret messages that don't involve invisible inks at all.

*Or will go batty trying to crack the code, which is just as good

SECRET MESSAGES IN PLAIN SIGHT

There are several ways of creating secret messages without resorting to invisible ink. Perhaps the cheekiest is to fill in a crossword.

Most newspapers and quite a few magazines feature crossword puzzles. Your message can be as long as the number of clues there are in the puzzle. Fill it in using the 'clues down' spaces only (which makes it even harder to read at a passing glance). For added security you can start with the last clue (say 28 down) and work backwards to the first.

If the space for the clue is longer than the first word of your message, continue with your message until you run out of space, then go on to the next clue down.

Whenwrittenoutthiswillleaveyouwithamessagewitho utpunctuationlikethisbutitcanstillbereadwithonlyalit tledifficulty.

Now fill in the clues across, using any words that fit and your secret message is in place. Since nobody bothers with a crossword that's already filled in, the chances of it being read by anybody other than your contact are slim. But if that's a worry, you can increase the level of security by alternating clues down with clues across in a prearranged pattern.

Once your crossword message is complete, you can deliver it using the old newspaper switch described earlier.

Another neat method of creating a secret message can also use a newspaper, but works quite well with books, magazines or other forms of printed text. All you need to make your message is a pin and a little patience. What you do is put a tiny pinhole underneath certain letters of an article so they spell out your message. The end result might be something like this:

The **Daily Blah**

China prayers answered!

The year 1333 opened badly in China. Drought in earlier years led to crop failure and famine. Everybody prayed for rain and in 1333 their prayers were answered ... with a flood that swept across the central plains and drowned 400,000 people.

The flooding was so great an entire mountain collapsed, leaving a gaping hole to show where it once stood.

Just twelve months later the drought came back. Locusts then ate up the last of the crops and there was famine again. Volcanoes started up. For nearly ten years, earthquake followed flood followed earthquake. Even for a country as used to disasters as China, it must have seemed like the end of the world.

You may have to strain your eyes to read it, but those two gloomy paragraphs contain a pinprick message reading, *can we meet soon.* Spotting real pinpricks is a lot easier once you know what you're looking for. Fold your newspaper or magazine to expose a single page at a time and hold it up to the light. The pinpricks will shine like beacons.

(An interesting variation on the pinprick method is to replace the pinpricks with dots of invisible ink. Even if a suspicious enemy checks for an invisible ink message, he's unlikely to notice such tiny markings ... or the message they spell out.)

Another – and extremely ancient – way of sending a secret message in plain sight requires a little preliminary preparation. As well as writing materials you need two round batons of exactly the same diameter. Give one baton to your contact, who will eventually use it as a decoder.

To create your message, cut your paper into a single long strip and wrap it carefully around your baton so the edges touch, but don't overlap. Secure it in place with an elastic band at each end. Now write your message, coded or in plain English depending on how secret you need to get, along the length of the baton.

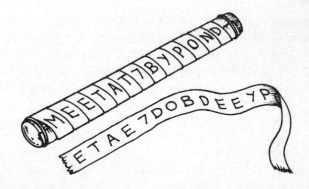

Although the message is perfectly clear while the paper remains in place, it turns into a meaningless jumble of letters once you unwrap the strip. And here's the ingenious bit: your message only reappears when the paper strip is wrapped around another baton the same size as the one you used to prepare it. A baton like the duplicate you've already given to your contact...

BHOGDQR

The heading of this section reads *Ciphers*. If you can't understand why, don't worry – you'll know that secret, and a good many others, by the time you finish reading the next few pages.

Morse

The most famous cipher of them all is Morse. (I know it's always called Morse *Code*, but that just goes to show the whole world can be just plain wrong sometimes.) Morse is a series of dots and dashes representing each letter of the alphabet. Although world famous, surprisingly few people actually know it – especially if you live inland – so any spy will find it well worth learning, especially when you add the extra layer of security I'll explain later. Here's how it goes:

A ● —	B — ● ● ●	C — ● — ●
D — ● ●	E ●	F ● ● — ●
G — — ●	H ● ● ● ●	I ● ●
J ● — — —	K — ● —	L ● — ● ●
M — —	N — ●	O — — —
P ● — — ●	Q — — ● —	R ● — ●
S ● ● ●	T —	U ● ● —
V ● ● ● —	W ● — —	X — ● ● —
Y — ● — —	Z — — ● ●	

You can produce a question mark (?) by going •• — — •• and make a full stop (.) with • — • — —.

The great thing about Morse is that you don't have to write it down (although you can). You can use it to send light or sound messages, which is a lot more than you can say for most ciphers. For example, if you're in a lighted room at night, all you need do is move the corner of a curtain to send a Morse message to somebody outside. Let the light shine out to a count of three to represent a dash, to the count of one to represent a dot. You can do much the same thing with an electric torch or even a mirror to reflect the sun in daytime.

Sound is even better since you can set up your message so only the right person is likely to hear it. Like a light signal, you can make a single tap represent a dot with three taps in quick succession as a dash. Or, if you want to be really cunning, the length of the gaps between taps can be your Morse signal. A count of one gap between taps is a dot, a count of three is a dash.

You can use Morse sound signals almost anywhere. You can tap a message on a wall for the benefit of somebody in the next room. Tapping on radiators or water pipes will carry the sound for surprising distances through a house. If you tap gently on a metal fence, your contact will be able to hear it by putting his ear to the fence even if he's quite a long way away. You can even hobble past

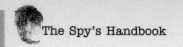

your contact, pretending to have a sprained ankle, and tap him out a quick message on the pavement with your crutch.

All this gives you an idea just how useful Morse can be, but it still has one big drawback. Even those who don't actually understand Morse will often recognize that a Morse signal is being sent – most people realize a pattern of dots and dashes means something. And all it takes for them to intercept your message next time is a quick glance in a Boy Scout handbook.

Unless, that is, you cipher your cipher.

Ciphering your Cipher

This is the second level of security I mentioned earlier and it's guaranteed hugely to confuse any Smart Alec with a knowledge of Morse who thinks he can cut himself in on your spying activities. The best way to show you how it works is with an example. Here's a simple message in Morse:

Not too difficult to decode using the key I gave you earlier — try it: I've added a slash between words to make it really easy. But when you've finished that one, try this:

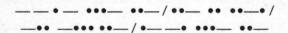

Not quite so easy this time. Even when you decipher the Morse, the message – QVU UIF DBU PVU – doesn't make much sense. But that's because I've added a second level of security by ciphering the cipher!

Actually what you have here is a message shifted one place forward in the alphabet. It's the most basic cipher there is and it probably wouldn't have fooled you for a minute if you hadn't been up to your neck in Morse. Here's the alphabet shifted one place forward, with the familiar alphabet directly underneath it:

BCDEFGHIJKLMNOPQRSTUVWXYZA
ABCDEFGHIJKLMNOPQRSTUVWXYZ

You can use that to decipher your second message, QVU UIF DBU PVU. Run your finger along the top line until you find the first letter of your message, which is Q. Now drop down onto the second line where you'll find the original, unshifted letter represented by Q, which is P. So the first letter of your message is actually P.

Now run your finger along the top line until you come to V and repeat the process. You'll find V represents U. Keep on keeping on and you'll quickly discover you're deciphering exactly the same message you had the first time, the only difference is the second level of security.

While the example given illustrates the principle, it's actually unlikely that you'd ever use anything so simple as a single forward shift. You can create far more complex shift ciphers very easily with the aid of an ingenious device invented by the French Military Academy during the nineteenth century. It's called a cipher slide and this is the way to make it:

The Cipher Slide

Take an ordinary A4 sheet of paper and trim a strip about the width of your thumb off one side. Write two complete alphabets on the strip, one after the other, like this:

ABCDEFGHIJKLMNOPQRSTUVWXYZABCD

EFGHIJKLMNOPQRSTUVWXYZ

Leave the strip to one side and write the alphabet again, once this time, left to right in the middle of your sheet of paper. Using scissors, cut two slits in the paper immediately underneath the alphabet you've just written, as shown on the next page.

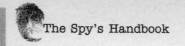
ABCDEFGHIJKLMNOPQRSTUVWXYZ

One slit should appear below and just before the A, the second below and just after the Z. Both should be a little larger than the width of your thumb.

To complete your cipher slide, thread the strip of paper with the double alphabet through the first of your slits, starting at the back of the paper and threading through to the front. Bring it across and thread it front to back through the second slit. If you've done it properly, you've now got a movable alphabet directly underneath the alphabet written on your sheet of paper. As you pull the strip backwards and forwards, different letters will line up.

Make a second cipher slide for a fellow spy and you can send each other secret messages by setting both slides to the same letter. If A is set to equal H, for example, you can quickly read off the equivalents of the remaining letters in order to create or decipher a message.

You can make matters even more secure by writing the letters on your strip in a completely random order. It'll still work provided both cipher slides have the same random order. Alternatively, you can replace the letters on the strip with numbers or a set of symbols you create. So long as both slides are the same, this allows you to produce secret messages that will utterly confuse your enemies.

You can do something very similar using your home computer, providing you and your friend have the same unusual font. The secret message may look like something out of Tutankhamen's tomb, but it's not actually Egyptian at all – just a plain old English language message written in a hieroglyphic computer font:

It's virtually impossible to decipher off the page* but if you and your fellow spy share the same font, you can decipher on screen simply by selecting the message and changing the font back to Times or Courier.

Keyword Cipher

You can add yet another level of security by introducing something called a keyword cipher. The key*word* can actually be a key *phrase*. Here's how it works – instead of writing a normal, standard ABC alphabet on the strip of paper you're going to thread through your cipher slide, create a special keyword alphabet. You do this by deciding on a keyword or short phrase which doesn't use any alphabet letter more than once. Write down that keyword to begin the alphabet on your strip, then fill in any letters you *haven't* used in their normal order immediately afterwards. Do this twice, so you have two complete (keyword) alphabets on the strip, much as you had before.

Let's suppose the keyword you picked was *Quickbrown* (I know it doesn't make sense – it doesn't have to). First you check to make sure you haven't duplicated any letters. Since you haven't, you should now write down the alphabet as follows:

QUICKBROWNADEFGHJLMPSTVXYZ

What you've done here is write QUICKBROWN followed by the rest of the letters of the alphabet that don't appear in the phrase QUICK BROWN. Now do it again, so what you have is a strip that reads:

**QUICKBROWNADEFGHJLMPSTVXYZQUI
CKBROWNADEFGHJLMPSTVXYZ**

*To put you out of your misery, it reads: There were spies in ancient Egypt too, you know!

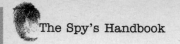

Feed that into your cipher slide and you have the makings of a very secure cipher, which you can change any time you want to just by changing the keyword. You send your cipher message to your fellow spy, then send him/her the keyword separately. Unless somebody knows your keyword, it's virtually impossible to decipher the message.

A variation on the theme is to substitute numbers (1 to 26) for the letters on your strip. They can be in any order you want, providing the spy who receives your message knows what that order is. One of my own favourite tricks is to lay out a number message so it looks like a complicated mathematical formula rather than just a row of numbers. That way, a lot of people don't even think to try to decipher it – they just assume it's boring old arithmetic and go on to something else.

YOUR ENIGMA MACHINE

The trouble with simply substituting one letter for another – or even a number for a letter – is that code breakers know certain letters come up more often than others in any message. The letter E, for example, is the most common letter in the English language. (Just look how often I've used it in this paragraph already!) So if a code breaker has a cipher message that's packed with, say, Bs, he knows that B is likely to equal E in the cipher and this gives him a clue to the way the other letters are substituted.

To try to get around this weakness, spies cast about for a way of continually changing which letter was substituted for another letter during a single message. So while B might equal E in the first word, Z could be substituted for E in the second. That way, the fact that E is the most common letter in any message would never show up. But when you continually change the letters you substitute, you have to let the recipient of the message know exactly what you've done otherwise they won't be able to read it. This is quite difficult to do without leaving traces and patterns a code breaker can use.

But way back in 1920, an American named Edward H. Hebern came up with a brilliant idea. He basically figured that what you do is build a special typewriter. In an ordinary typewriter, hitting a key causes the letter on that key to be printed on a piece of paper. But in Hebern's typewriter, every key had an electric rotor between it and

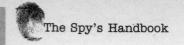

the paper and every rotor had the whole of the alphabet and all the usual punctuation marks on it.

When you hit the E key (or any other key) on a machine like this, the rotor spins so that you might print a K on the paper, or a Q or an S or a full stop or even (sometimes) an E! Hit the E key again and a completely different letter is printed. Since this happens with every letter on your keyboard, you just type away and your message is neatly ciphered for you.

Furthermore, it's ciphered in such a way that it's almost impossible for an enemy spy to crack - especially if you put more rotors behind your first rotors. But your recipient can read your message easily...provided he has a special Hebern typewriter set up in the same way as yours. All he does is type in your ciphered message, spin the rotors in reverse and there it is, in plain text, all neatly printed out.

Rotor-driven cipher typewriters were also built in Europe and improved over the years until, about ten years later, the Germans perfected the most famous of all cipher machines, Enigma. They used it to code all their secret messages from about 1930 onwards and, convinced its product was unbreakable, continued to use it throughout the World War Two.

Your D-I-Y Enigma

Making yourself a full-scale electronic Enigma machine might prove a little tricky, not to mention costly, but you can certainly use the basic rotor principle to create a neat device that will help you generate virtually unbreakable ciphers. Here's how:

Find yourself a nice big piece of plain light card and use a pair of compasses to draw three circles on it. Make the second about 2.5 cm in diameter larger than the first. Make the third about 2.5 cm in diameter larger than the second. Draw a pencil line through the exact centre of each. With this as a guide, use a protractor from your school geometry class to help you mark 12° divisions right around the edge of each circle. Cut out the circles

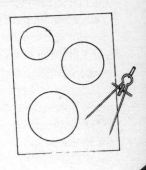

Once you've done that, use a ruler to join each of your 12° division marks to the centre of the circle. You'll be left with something that looks like a pie divided into thirty slices. Do this for all three discs.

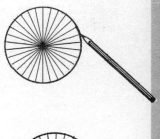

On the largest of the three discs, write the numbers 1 to 30 along the outer edge, with one number appearing in each of the divisions you've just made. You don't have to write them in order – in other words it can be something like 15, 8, 22, 4, 17 and so on – but do make sure you use all 30 numbers. On the smallest disc, write the letters of the alphabet. Since there are only 26 letters in the

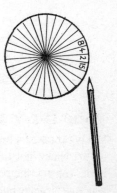

alphabet, this will leave you with four divisions blank. Put a full stop in one of them, the word YES in another, the word NO in a third. The last blank division can be left blank to represent a space.

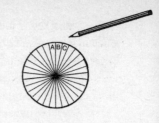

On the medium-sized disc, alternate a letter with a number (starting with A, then 1, then B, then 2 and so on) in each of the divisions until you run out of spaces, which will happen when you reach the number 15, just after the letter Q.

Make a small hole through the centre of each disc using a ball-point or sharp pencil, then join all three discs together using one of those split pins you push through and open up at the back. What you have now is your personal, portable, pocket-sized Enigma machine composed of three superimposed discs, each of which can be moved independently of the others.

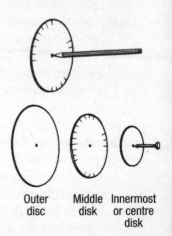

Outer disc   Middle disk   Innermost or centre disk

Make an identical Enigma for each member of your spy ring. Now you're ready to go into the cipher business big time.

To create a secret message, you need to set your Enigma. Since this is the first time you've used it, I'll make things simple by ignoring the middle disc for the moment. Turn the small disc so that the letter A lines up with a number on the outer disc. It can be any one of the numbers, but be sure to make a note of which one.

You'll notice once you line up A, all the other letters of the alphabet, plus the YES/NO spaces, the full stop and the space all line up with numbers as well. Now write out the message you want to send and use your Enigma to read off the numbers that correspond to the letters in your message. Add in any full stops and spaces by entering the numbers for those as well.

The end result will be a line of numbers that don't make any sense to anybody. You can separate them out with commas, but apart from that, there won't even be a space between them.

To let the members of your spy ring know how to decipher your message, all you need to tell them is how to set their own Enigma discs; and you can do that very easily indeed. Suppose you set your wheel with A lined up to the number 7. Make the first number of your message 7 and your spies know they have to set their Enigma discs to A=7. Once they've done that, deciphering is easy – they simply read the numbers in your message back to their relevant letters.

If you think it may be a bit too obvious making 7 the first number of your message, you can make it the last number, or the third number, or the seventeenth, just so long as your spies know where to find the key. You can even send it separately. If you're posting the message, write it under the stamp.

So where does the third disc come in? That's there to make super-safe ciphers. Set your inner and outer discs exactly as before, but this time set the middle disc as well, once again lining up a number or a letter with the central-disc letter A. Once again keep careful note of your settings.

Now when you cipher your message, alternate letter by letter between the centre and the outer disc. This time your end result will be a jumble of numbers and letters just about impossible to crack without a personal Enigma and the key.

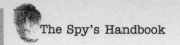

In this case the key is a bit more complicated than the example given earlier. You have to let your spies know what A equals in both the middle and the outer discs. Then you have also to tell them whether to start alternating with the middle disc or the outer disc. Sounds difficult, but it isn't.

Suppose you set A on the innermost disc opposite the letter U on the middle disc and the number 12 on the outer disc. And also suppose you decided to start the first letter of your message by reading from the middle disc, then alternating outer disc, middle disc, outer disc etc. until the message is completely ciphered.

To convey all that information to your spies, you need simply start your message with the following:

12,U,M

This means A = 12 on the outer disc, A = U on the middle disc and you should start with the middle disc (M for middle) when you alternate between middle and outer discs for the deciphering. If you'd started with the outer disc, then the start of your message would read 12,U,O (for outer).

Try it. It's a lot more simple than it sounds, but the resulting cipher would give trouble to the FBI.

CODES

Ciphers are handy because you can use them to send any message you want. Although infinitely more difficult to crack, codes are far less flexible. That's sort of obvious once you start to think about it. With a cipher, you only need 26 different symbols – one for every letter of the alphabet. With a code, you need a different symbol for every word you use and there are millions of words in the English language.

But before you throw codes out the window, there's something you should know. Although there are millions of words in the English language, most of us only use a few hundred of them in everyday conversation.

And if even a few hundred seems too much, then consider this: when you send a message to a spy, you won't waste time talking about the weather – you'll keep it tight and sharp and to the point. Many of the messages you'll want to send are standard anyway and messages such as this can be coded in their entirety *with a single symbol*. Without a code book to interpret them, nobody, but nobody can have the least idea what those symbols mean.

So while most of your secret messages will be in cipher, you should take a little time to develop your own code book for emergencies. It's very easy to do. Simply work out a series of words and phrases you think you're most likely to use and dream up a different symbol to represent each of them. Here are a few ideas:

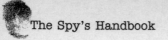

URGENT!	ⅢⅢ▶
TODAY	●
TOMORROW	●●
NEXT WEEK	●●●
NEXT MONTH	●●●●
NEXT YEAR	●●●●●
AT ONCE	▶◀
FOR YOUR EYES ONLY	◉◉
YOUR COVER IS BLOWN	💣
MY COVER IS BLOWN	💣
STOP ALL SPYING OPERATIONS UNTIL FURTHER NOTICE	⃠
MESSAGE WAITING AT THE DROP	✕
COME HOME, ALL IS FORGIVEN	🏠
REPORT TO UNCLE	👓

YOU ARE BEING WATCHED

I'M MADLY IN LOVE WITH YOU

LEAVE TOWN AT ONCE

BRING ME MONEY

REPORT FOR YOUR NEXT ASSIGNMENT

I NEED TO HEAR FROM YOU

YOUR DISGUISE IS READY

END YOUR SURVEILLANCE OPERATION

ENEMY DEFEATED

JOB NOW FINISHED

YOU'RE A USELESS BLUEBOTTLE

YOU'VE BEEN PROMOTED

YOU'VE BEEN DEMOTED

YOU'RE SACKED

NEVER DARKEN MY SPY RING AGAIN

RECRUIT A NEW AGENT

Remember you need to make two code books – one for you, one for the recipient of your messages. Use code symbols as if they were ornamentation or doodles in ordinary (innocent) notes or letters. You might draw one in the margin of an exercise book, then loan the book to a member of your spy ring. If you want to be really clever, you might drop one or two into a ciphered message. Your enemies will be so busy trying to crack the cipher they'll never even get started on the code.

The really big danger of using this type of code is the possibility that a copy of your code book may fall into the wrong hands. Once that happens, every message you send might as well be broadcast by the BBC. Fortunately there's another method of coding, based on a completely different principle, still widely used by professional spies and, with a little care, just about impossible to crack. It's called book coding and the way it works is this.

You and the person who will receive your messages must first of all agree on the book you're going to use. It can be anything you like from a popular novel to a dictionary and the only thing you need to be sure of is that you're both using the same edition.

To create your message, you simply find the words you need within the pages of the book. Note them down in the form of page number, followed by line number, followed by a number that tells you the position of the word in the line. Here's an example taken from a modern edition of Samuel Pepys' Diary:*

119,3,2/ 294,10,7/569,1,4/438,1,3/501,10,1

If you happen to have a copy of that edition handy, you can decode the message by turning to page 119, counting down to the third line and noting the second word. Then on to page 294, line 10, seventh word, then page 569, line one, fourth word and so on until the message is complete.

(If you don't happen to have a copy of the edition handy it doesn't matter – it's only an example message which reads, *Go to London in July.*)

*The Shorter Pepys, selected and edited by Robert Latham, Penguin Books, London, 1987

Once you start working with this sort of code, you quickly realize you can send messages about anything in a form that simply can't be intercepted unless the code breaker knows the book you're using.

A really good approach is to use a book from your local library. That way the recipient can borrow the same book, thus making sure you're both using the same edition. For added security, you can vary the book – all you have to do is let your contact know.

INFORMATION GATHERING

It's all very well being able to pass on information in code or cipher, but a good spy needs to know how to get the information in the first place. In all the spy movies you'll ever see, this involves breaking and entering, blowing up safes, photographing documents, bugging, kidnapping, shooting people and getting into exciting car chases. Which is all very well if you've got the time, but frankly there are a lot easier ways of collecting information.

Listening

One of the simplest is just listening. I know that sounds so obvious it's almost dumb, but next time you see two people talking watch exactly what they're doing. I'll guarantee that nine times out of ten, both of them will be talking and neither of them will be really listening. Sometimes they'll actually talk at the same time. Most times one will be waiting impatiently for the other to shut up.

The plain fact is most people know how to talk, but very few know how to listen.

Listening – good listening – is actually an art form. But fortunately it's one you can quickly develop. Next time you get into a conversation, forget about all the things you're just dying to say and let the other person open up. That means three things:

First, ask questions. How are *you* today? What have you been doing? What's your news? Did you win your match? Did you pass your exam? What do you think about...? Did you meet anybody nice? Where are you going? Your end of the conversation should be peppered with question marks and the word 'you'.

Next, keep your mouth shut. Having encouraged somebody to talk with questions, let them get on with it. Don't interrupt (except possibly to ask a clarifying question). Don't leap in with your own opinions. Don't start arguments. Just keep quiet.

Finally, encourage the flow. That means making a real effort to be interested and to stay interested. Watch the other person's mouth while he talks. Resist the urge to float off in a daydream. Nod encouragingly at intervals. Smile at the jokes, laugh at the good ones, allow yourself a soft *'Wow, cool'* when you're impressed. In other words, show the other person you really, truly, deeply appreciate the things they're saying.

That little three-way guide is all you need to turn yourself into a good listener – that and a lot of practice. But once you get the hang of it, several unexpected things will happen.

The first is that your popularity will soar. More and more people will want to talk to you. Next – and this is really weird – people will start describing you as a good *talker*. I know this doesn't make sense, but believe me it will happen. Next, you'll get a reputation as somebody with a lot of intelligence and common sense, probably because you've stopped forcing your dumb opinions down people's throats. But most important of all, you'll discover lots of people are prepared to trust you with their deepest secrets. That's good news for a spy.

Ask Questions

Becoming a good listener is an excellent way of collecting information, but it's *passive*. You have to take what's offered and sometimes what's offered isn't the thing you're most interested in for your espionage assignment. So how do you get people to tell you the thing you most want to know? Here again the answer is deceptively simple: you just ask.

For many people that's just *too* simple. You're probably familiar with this sort of situation. You want to know whether Jean has started dating Joe. The simplest way to find out would be to ask Jean or Joe (preferably Jean, since Joe tends to boast a lot). But then this dialogue starts up in your head. Jean would never tell me that. She's a very private person. She'd say it was none of my business. So it's not worth asking.

This sort of self-censorship stops an amazing number of questions from being asked. Yet experience will quickly teach you that if you ask somebody a direct, simple question – however personal – as often as not, they will give you an honest answer. (This is especially true if you've developed a reputation as a good listener and, above all, somebody who knows how to keep a secret.)

The point about all this is that if you *don't* ask the question, there's no chance you'll be told what you want to know. Whereas if you *do* ask the question, you'll get a straight answer at least 50% of the time. And even a refusal to answer can be useful. Did the person you asked look shifty? Did the question make them nervous? Angry? Sullen? Very often, such emotional reactions can give you clues to what's going on. This isn't as good as finding out the full facts, but for a spy it's better than nothing.

Once you go beyond passive listening and straightforward questioning, you step into the interesting area of interrogation techniques.

Forget the bright light and the rubber hose – that sort of nonsense is best left to Hollywood. In a really skilled interrogation, the subject doesn't even know it's happening to him. Here are a few tips on how to conduct the sort of subtle interrogation that will get results:

 Be patient. A skilled interrogation takes time. Lots of time.

 Get friendly. A friend is far more likely to tell you what you want to know than a stranger, so your first job is to turn the stranger into a friend. Use your well-known charm and recently developed skills as a good listener. Take your time and don't bring up the subject that interests you until things are really cosy.

 Be patient. Give it enough time and the person might tell you what you want to know of his or her own accord.

 Guide the conversation.

 Be patient.

Added to those five points is an important sixth – people will often tell you more by what they *don't* say than by what they do. You'll find out how when you study one of a spy's most important information-gathering tools: body language.

BODY LANGUAGE

A friend once gave me directions to a chip shop with the words, 'Straight down the street, then take the first on your right.' As she did so, she gestured with her left hand. She caught the look on my face and grinned. 'Follow my hand, not my mouth,' she told me. I went down the street, took the first on the left and found my chip shop.

Although nothing to do with spying, this little incident is an interesting example of what's called body language. Experts are convinced that up to 93% of all communication between human beings doesn't involve words. It's a mixture of voice tones, eye movements, body postures, hand gestures, leg movements, facial expressions, voice volume, twitches, itches, sniffs, teeth grinding and a whole lot more. What's more, like my friend's hand gesture, body language is usually a far more accurate indicator of what's going on than any words spoken.

Take the simple instruction *come here*. Those two words can mean a lot of different things, depending on the body language.

☞ If they're delivered as a shout – "COME HERE!!" – they really mean, 'Come here *at once*.'

☞ If they're whispered softly with a sidelong glance, they mean, 'Come here, I want to kiss you.'

☞ If the voice is cold and the face is frowning, they can mean, 'Come here for your punishment, you brat.'

☞ If the eyes are looking through a window and the tone is excited, you can be sure they mean, 'Come here, I want to show you something.'

Not only can you figure out what a person is really saying by watching their body language, but you can strongly influence the way they feel, react and behave by the body language you exhibit yourself.

The Crowded Lift

Try this experiment next time you enter a crowded lift. Instead of stepping into the lift then turning to face the door as you usually do (and as everybody else has done) just stand facing the other people. After a second or two, you'll notice them beginning to grow tense and nervous. If you want to increase the tension, grin at them. By the time the lift reaches its destination, they'll be glaring at you crossly ... all because your body language didn't suit the situation you were in.

Where's The Coin?

Any spy who has made a study of body language is way ahead of the posse when it comes to an interrogation. She is usually able to tell quite easily when subjects are lying and with a little practice may also be able to guess the information they're trying to hide. Try the old 'which hand holds the coin?' trick. Hand somebody a coin, tell them to put their hands behind their back and switch the coin at random into their left or right hand. Then have them bring both hands back to the front and try to guess which hand holds the coin.

At first, you'll just be guessing, so you'll only be right about half the time. But start looking for subtle body signals. After a while you may discover he leans slightly towards the hand with the coin in it. Or he may hold that hand a little higher (or a little lower) than the other. He may even point to the coin hand with his nose. Once you spot the signal, it'll tell you where the coin is every time – and mystify your friend so long as you don't tell him you're watching his body language.

Doing It Blindfold

A variation on the coin trick that's a lot more spooky than guessing the hand is to have a group of people hide your coin somewhere in the room while you're outside. Tell them that wherever they hide it, you will be able to find it using the psychic powers you developed as an espionage agent working on the X-Files. Don't mention body language since this information can be used to block the trick.

The group should then pick someone to blindfold you and lead you into the room. Ask the person to hold your arm gently and walk around the room with you, making sure you don't trip or hurt yourself by bumping into something. Then begin criss-crossing the room until you 'miraculously' find your coin.

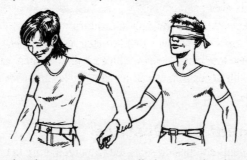

This trick takes practice as well, but it's also based on body language. Once you're blindfold, concentrate on the pressure of your guide's hand on your arm. She won't even realize she's doing it, but she will unconsciously try to push you away whenever you get close to the hidden coin. It's a very subtle thing, but once you spot it, you can locate the coin by simply moving against the push. You might also usefully listen to her breathing and the breathing of anybody else within earshot. It will tend to speed up as you reach the coin.

While a full study of body language could take years, here are some tips to get you started.

Look At The Eyes

Eyes can communicate more information than any other part of the body. If your subject maintains eye contact with you during an interrogation, it can suggest he's trustworthy. But shifty eyes and too much blinking can point to deception. Relaxed, comfortable eye movements in a subject who's attentive might lead you to believe he's honest and sincere.

But that's just a broad background principle. You have to watch for sudden changes in eye-movement behaviour. If a shifty individual abruptly looks you in the eye and holds your gaze, it doesn't mean he's decided to tell the truth for once – it's much more likely to mean he's about to lie in his teeth and wants desperately to convince you otherwise.

It can work the other way round as well. If someone who has been looking at you steadily suddenly looks away, chances are he's decided to lie about something.

Eye movements aren't the only indicators you need to look for. Watch out for little shrugs, hand-to-face gestures, playing with (or even just touching) nearby objects, all of which can all be associated with deception, as can lengthy pauses and over or under explanations.

Movement and Posture

Body movements and postures can tell you much more than whether or not somebody's lying. The following table – which is worth learning by heart – will give you some idea of what to watch out for:

What To Look For	What It Means
Arms crossed over the chest	The person is feeling defensive. This is a particularly strong sign in a woman.
Nail biting	Nervousness or insecurity.
Brisk walk	Indicates confidence, particularly if the person holds him/herself erect and upright.
Hand goes to cheek	The person is thinking, probably evaluating the situation.
Hands clasped behind the back	This can signal apprehension, frustration or even anger. (But doesn't apply if you're spying on Prince Charles – he only does it through force of habit.)
Head in hand, eyes down	You're looking at somebody who's bored out of their mind.
Looking down with the face turned away from you	The person doesn't believe what you're saying.
Open hands	Usually sincerity. Can sometimes be a sign of innocence.
Hair patting	The person – usually a woman – lacks confidence generally or may be feeling insecure in the particular situation.
Eyes close, pinches bridge of the nose	They don't think much of what you're saying.
Ear tugging	The person can't decide about something.

What To Look For	What It Means
Brisk hand rubbing	The person is looking forward eagerly to something. (But can also mean they're very cold.)
Eye rubbing	Usually disbelief or at least some doubt.
Seated legs crossed, hands clasped behind head	The person is feeling confident, maybe over-confident.
Legs crossed, one foot kicking slightly	They're bored.
Hands on hips	The person is ready for action, may even be feeling aggressive.
Chin stroking	The person is trying to come to a decision.
Drumming fingers	Impatience or nervousness.
Head tilt	Usually interest.
Nose touch or nose rub	The person is in doubt about something or lying.

HONEY TRAPS

A knowledge of body language can be of great use to a spy in one important area of espionage other than interrogation. This area is the honey trap.

A honey trap, you will recall from 'Learning the Lingo', at the beginning of the book, is set up when a spy persuades a target subject to fall in love with him or her in order to obtain information or co-operation. Which is all very well, but how do you go about persuading somebody to fall in love with you?

The answer – or at least part of the answer – is the use of romantic body language, or RBL. RBL differs from the body language we've just been examining in that all its signs and signals are associated with courtship. A knowledge of RBL allows you to send out your own silent signals of interest in the target, while reading clearly whether she/he is interested in you.

The first thing to realize about RBL is that women can generally spot romantic signals more easily than men. Possibly because of this awareness, women have, over the years, developed far more RBL signals than men, although there are certain signs that are common to both sexes.

So how do you know when somebody is ripe to walk into a honey trap? In other words, how do you know when someone fancies you? Just keep a weather eye out for these wordless signals, all of which suggest an interest:

If You're A Girl ...

The target straightens his jacket, coat, shirt, tie or other item of clothing when you approach. (This is known as 'preening behaviour' and suggests he wants to look his best for you.)

The target rubs a hand across his hair.

The target holds your gaze longer than usual.

The target stares deeply into your eyes.

The target hooks his thumbs into his belt, hands pointing downwards.

The target stands with his hands on his hips. (This is a tricky signal since it can also mean aggression. But between a man and a woman, it's usually a sign of interest, particularly if there are other RBL signs displayed.)

The target points his foot towards you.

When seated, the target sits with his legs spread.

If You're A Boy ...

The target tosses her hair.

The target's cheeks take on a slight flush.

The target holds your gaze long enough for you to notice then looks quickly away.

The target holds her arms in such a way that you can see the insides of her wrists.

The target gestures in such a way that the palms of her hands are visible.

The target holds her mouth slightly open.

The target's lips appear wet.

The target licks her lips.

The target has a tendency to speak more softly than usual.

When you catch her eye, the target glances downwards before looking away.

When Seated ...

The target tucks one leg under the other and sits so that her knee points towards you.

The target twines her legs together. (This is different from simply crossing her legs, although some women cross and uncross their legs frequently when in the presence of a man they like.)

The target plays with her shoe, allowing it to dangle from her foot or pulling it on and off.

For Either Sex ...

The first and most obvious signal is a smile. But since most people smile from pure habit it's useful to be able to tell the genuine smile from the fake. Don't look at the mouth – look at the eyes. If there is little or no wrinkling at the outer edges of the eyes, you may suspect the smile is phony.

Other Common Signals

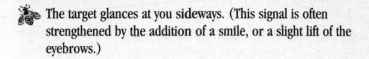 The target glances at you sideways. (This signal is often strengthened by the addition of a smile, or a slight lift of the eyebrows.)

The target keeps glancing towards you. (A shy target will sometimes pretend to be only looking in your general direction, but will surreptitiously look at you when he/she thinks you won't notice.)

The target holds your gaze, if only briefly. This signal can be quite subtle.

The target's eyes narrow slightly.

The target shows a more alert posture.

The target's body turns towards you or, during a conversation, you notice that the target's body posture matches your own.

During conversation the target's head tilts. This can also be a sign of interest in the conversation itself, but when someone is interested in your conversation you can generally take it they're at least somewhat interested in you.

The target's eyes brighten.

The target adjusts his/her hair.

In either sex the expansion of the pupils of the eyes is the strongest possible sign of interest in the person they're speaking to – and a sign that's almost impossible to fake.

While the signals explained in the past two chapters will usually apply to anybody you're likely to meet, it's as well to bear in mind that there are differences in the way certain nationalities interpret wordless signals.

For example, Asians, Puerto Ricans, West Indians and Native Americans are among those who consider direct eye contact rude and this will have an effect on the way they express early interest in a member of the opposite sex.

The thumbs-up sign, which signals approval in the British Isles and America, is a rude gesture in Nigeria and just denotes the number one in Germany and Japan. Making a circle with your thumb and finger denotes everything is OK when used in America and Britain, but in France people interpret it as zero, in Japan it denotes coinage, while in Brazil, Germany and Russia, it's a very rude gesture indeed.

Even something as simple as nodding or shaking your head can be tricky. In most Western countries a nod means yes, a shake means no, but quite the opposite interpretation is given in Iran, Turkey, Yugoslavia, Bulgaria, Bengal and parts of Greece.

Finally, any spy planning a honey trap needs to know when his or her fascinating good looks and internationally known charms simply aren't working. Watch out for the following non-verbal signs that indicate your target isn't interested:

Your target never so much as sneaks a peek at you. Any accidental eye contact causes the target to look away quickly, eyes level.

The target turns his/her body away from you.

The target's head remains upright during conversation.

The target's posture is unchanged and there is no preening behaviour.

The target's mouth remains closed except when speaking.

The target's body sags. (This signal is particularly relevant to a woman target.)

Generally speaking, an absence of positive signals can be taken as an indication that your target isn't interested in you and a honey trap would be very difficult to set up.

BEATING A LIE DETECTOR

The big thing about body language for a spy is not just knowing when somebody's lying to you – it's using it to lie to them. Even people who haven't studied body language instinctively react to the gestures and postures that usually accompany an honest statement of the truth.

Once you know what those body signs are – as you now do from the last two sections – you can consciously adopt truthful body language while you're lying in your teeth. The person you're lying to will find you hugely persuasive.

Unless, that is, they happen to have a lie detector.

The first lie detector was invented in 1904 by a character named Max Wertheimer, who started work on the device while he was still a student and finished it just after he received his doctorate from the University of Würzburg in Germany.

Wertheimer went on to become one of the founders of Gestalt psychology. His lie detector went on to become one of the more useful tools of policemen and spymasters throughout the world and particularly in the United States where they're even prepared to accept lie detector readings as evidence in court.

These days, lie detectors are called polygraphs, a word that gives you more than a passing hint of how they work. Poly comes from the Greek and means 'many'. Graph also comes from the Greek and while the original meaning was 'writing', it now denotes something that records. So a polygraph is a machine that records many things.

Specifically the many things a polygraph records are your pulse rate, your blood pressure, your rate of breathing and sometimes the rate at which your skin conducts electricity, known technically as your GSR or galvanic skin response. The reason it records these things is that they all show when you're lying.

The theory goes like this – if you're being interrogated and decide to tell a lie, you get stressed in case you're found out. Stress causes your pulse rate, blood pressure and breathing to rise, while your GSR increases. These are all natural, automatic reactions and once you get stressed, they happen completely unconsciously, hence outside your control.

When you're subjected to a polygraph test, the first thing they do after hooking you up is to ask a series of really dumb questions like, 'Is it raining right now?' or 'Who's the current President of the United States?' They watch the print-out as you answer these and after a couple of minutes they have your baseline rate – the readings that indicate you're not especially stressed and telling the truth.

Once they've got your baseline, they hit you with the 'Where did you hide the stolen documents?' sort of question and watch how far the readings jump above baseline to find out whether you're telling the truth when you answer.

Sounds as if they've got you taped, but as a good spy (who's read this handbook) you know you can beat the polygraph any time you want to. There are two or three ways of doing it.

Use The Mantra

The first is the use of a mantra. A mantra is a word or phrase you can repeat over and over in your mind until it blanks out everything else. Remember that the reactions they're recording are all caused by the stress levels experienced in your mind. Calm your mind and you calm the stress. Calm the stress and you calm your body. Calm your body and the lie detector has nothing to detect.

A good mantra, repeated over and over, is the poem *Twinkle, Twinkle, Little Star*.

Condition Your Reflexes

The second way to beat the polygraph is to set up a conditioned reflex. Conditioned reflexes were discovered by a Russian psychologist named Pavlov. In a series of experiments he presented his hungry dogs with food (which made their mouths water) and rang a bell at the same time. After he'd done this around seventy times, he tried ringing the bell without presenting the food. Sure enough, the dogs' mouths still watered. Pavlov decided the salivation reflex had become conditional on the bell, not the food. A small mistake in translation meant we now talk about conditioned reflexes rather than the conditional reflexes he originally reported.

You can set up a conditioned reflex the same way Pavlov did. To beat the polygraph, the reflex you want to set up is one of deep relaxation. Listen to calming music, get yourself comfortable, take deep breaths until you're as peaceful and floppy as it's possible to get. Then set up your conditioning trigger. This could be something as simple as the word *calm* mentally repeated three times in succession.

Keep practising. It takes more than one shot to set up a conditioned reflex. But every time you relax deeply, repeat those three words, *calm…calm…calm*. Do this long enough and you'll find that by simply repeating *calm…calm…calm* will send you into a deeply relaxed state. Hit the *calm…calm…calm* button when they wire you up to a polygraph and your body won't react to the questions however much you lie – and nor will the machine.

The trouble with these two methods is that mantras take a lot of concentration while conditioned reflexes have to be set up firmly in advance. But the third method of beating the lie detector will work even if you're seized in a dawn raid and can hardly think straight.

Get Excited

This method involves artificially raising your baseline rate. All you do is wait until they start asking you those dumb initial questions about the weather, then visualise yourself vividly in a high excitement situation. You might, for example, imagine yourself driving a fast car around a racetrack or meeting your favourite pop star.

The result will be a baseline reading so high that when you stop visualising, the peaks that arise when you're lying will never show.

INFORMATION SOURCES

If, for some reason, you can't get the information you want directly from the person concerned, there are still a couple of places where you can collect a surprising amount of data in return for just a little effort.

Your Library

The first is your local library. Yeah, yeah, I know – fuddy-duddy old library. Who wants to waste their time in a place like that when they could be outside playing footie? But believe me, with an attitude like that, you'll never make a master spy. Libraries are great information sources once you pull your head out of the fiction section long enough to look around properly.

The trick is to know how to use your library. It's no use browsing vaguely in the hope you'll trip over the information you want. Check the relevant section carefully. Learn how to use the indexing system. (It's not all that hard.) Ask the library staff for help. And above all remember that the books on the shelves are just the tip of a very large iceberg. Any library worth its salt can order you virtually any book in print on any subject under the sun – and quite a few books that are out of print as well. You may have to wait a week or two for it to arrive, but that's the only drawback.

Get Surfing

The second source of information is the Internet. Start with one of the big search engines. I like Google best (http://www.google.com) but you'll get excellent results from any of the following:

http://uk.yahoo.com
http://www.lycos.co.uk
http://altavista.co.uk
http://www.excite.co.uk
http://www.askjeeves.co.uk
http://www.northernlight.com

It's also possible to use what they call meta-engines – search engines that call on a whole load of other search engines and give you the results collected from each. Examples of meta-engines are:

http://www.ixquick.com
http://www.dogpile.com
http://www.zworks.com

I'm not really keen on meta-engines – I find with many of them that you waste a lot of time ploughing through endless duplicated results – but you should try them for yourself to discover whether or not they suit your style.

If you've never used a search engine before, you'll be pleasantly surprised by how easy it is. Just log on to the search site of your choice and type a keyword (for example, 'spying') in the box provided. Then click the search button and wait. In a very short space of time you'll be presented with a long list of websites that contain the keyword you've selected.

At this point you'll suddenly realize the first drawback to using the Internet as an information source. The list is likely to be hundreds, maybe even thousands, of entries long. And you have to click on each of them, wait for the site to load, then scan through the content, before you can tell what information it contains.

Which will bring you to the second and third drawbacks of the Internet in very quick succession. Having opened a promising site, you may easily discover no more than a passing mention of the information you need. Conversely, you may find so much information that you don't have time to sift through it for what you want.

Finally, and most importantly, you'll quickly discover the Internet is jam-packed with utter rubbish – inaccurate, misleading and sometimes downright batty texts pretending to be kosher information.

There's not much you can do about the first three drawbacks, but you certainly have to do something about the last one. For a spy, inaccurate information is worse than no information at all. The only way to be certain is to use reliable sources. If you want information on space travel, go to NASA (http://www.nasa.gov) not http://www.amateurflyingsaucerbuilder.com. If you want to check facts about the past, try the British Museum at http://www.thebritishmuseum.ac.uk. For the official story, go to official sites (but remember the official story may be lies). For hard facts, check the reputable encyclopaedias – there are lots of them on-line.

If you save your pennies, you can even buy software that will search out information for you, often connecting with little-known sites in the process. These applications claim to be able to…

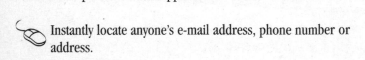 Instantly locate anyone's e-mail address, phone number or address.

Get copies of FBI files.

Check driving and criminal records.

Locate old classmates, a missing person or a long-lost love.

Investigate family histories to give details of births, marriages, divorces and deaths.

They work particularly well in the United States where the Freedom of Information Act allows you to dig the dirt legally on just about anybody or any thing. The UK and Europe have different ideas about the value of privacy, so some types of information are far harder to find. But even so, you can go a long way – legally – on the Internet so long as you're not actually living in a dictatorship. All it really needs is a little imagination and a lot of patience.

THE ART OF EAVESDROPPING

Of course there's some information you can't get by asking, you won't get by interrogation and isn't available in any library or Internet site. Which means it's time to turn sneaky with a little discreet eavesdropping.

Eavesdropping is an art. It's no good simply sauntering up to the conversation you want to overhear – once they see you coming, they'll start to talk about the weather. The prime rule of eavesdropping is that it must be carried out unseen and undetected. Let me give you an example of what I mean.

Magic?!

Several years ago, a stage conjurer told me he'd developed telepathy with his wife. When I expressed disbelief, he offered to prove it to me.

The 'proof' took the form of a card trick. The conjurer and I went for a stroll in the grounds of his home while his wife stayed in the house to make some coffee. I drew a card (the ten of clubs, as I recall) from a deck the conjurer produced. We had the usual chat about whether I wanted to change it, then the conjurer sent me back to the house. I went alone, of course, to make sure there were no secret signs. As I walked through the door, the wife handed me a cup of coffee and told me the card in my pocket was the ten of clubs.

At first I thought it had to be a trick deck, but the next day the conjurer repeated the experiment with a deck I brought and was no less successful. Then he pulled off the same trick without using cards at all. He asked me to name my favourite colour. Back at the house, his wife knew it. Then he asked the full name of my maternal grandmother. His wife knew it.

Then a city anywhere on Earth, then any number between 1 and 18,000, then the name I planned to give my next cat. His wife knew them all.

Then came the most mystifying bit. The conjurer blandly announced we had carried out so many successful experiments that he was now in direct telepathic communication with me. He handed me a pad and pen. "I'm going for a drive in my car," he said. "Wait until I'm out of sight, then write down the first phrase that comes into your head. Whisper the words as you do so, since that helps send the telepathic impression. Now this is important. When you've written the phrase down, tear out the page and burn it so you know I can't possibly find some way to look at it. In fact, burn the whole pad in case you've left an impression of the writing on the pages underneath."

I watched him start up his car and drive off.

When he was out of sight, I wrote down, *The eagle soars to heaven, but fox terriers wear three-piece suits.* (I know it's nonsense – I just wanted to make sure I wrote something he couldn't guess.) Then I burned the pad, page and all, on an outdoor barbecue. A couple of minutes later, the car drew up again and my conjurer friend handed me a drawing he'd made of a dog in a three-piece suit with a large bird flying above its head.

I went half mad trying to figure out how he did it, but the answer proved to be simple. The conjurer had bugged me.* The pen I used to write down the three-piece suit phrase was a cunningly disguised radio transmitter. It picked up the words I whispered 'to help the telepathic impression' and broadcast them. Any radio set within half a mile could pick them up if it was tuned to the right frequency. The conjurer had simply switched on his car radio. Earlier, the pen had been in his breast pocket, picking up our conversations about my favourite colour and the card I'd chosen. His wife had the kitchen radio on while she was making the coffee.

"I bought it in a spy shop," the conjurer told me proudly as he took back his pen.

Spy Shops

You might wonder where on earth the conjurer found a spy shop, but they're a lot more common than you might imagine. You should discover at least one somewhere in any large city and you'll find loads of them on the Internet. The three URLs on the next page will start you off but a search will bring up many more:

*In more ways than one!

http://www.spy-store.co.uk/
http://www.kopes.com/gadgets/spygadgets.htm
http://www.spystuff.com/products.html

Get Bugging

It won't take you long to find you can buy a pen bug like the one my conjurer used for £59.99. It's powered by two watch batteries and, as I discovered, 'can pick up the slightest whisper up to 12 metres away'. If you need something more sneaky, there's a room transmitter built into a working two-way mains adaptor. You just plug it in and any conversation that takes place in the room is yours for the listening and £39.99. A paltry £124.84 gets one with a built-in recorder. As a bonus, neither version needs a battery – both draw power directly from the mains.

These items may all seem a bit pricey if you're still at school, but shop around and you should be able to find something closer to your budget. There's a small, high-powered room transmitter about the size of two sugar cubes, for example, that will only set you back £24.99. It'll pick up sounds as far away as 15 metres and transmit them over a 100-metre distance.

Assuming you're prepared to buy from the United States, you'll discover an aid to eavesdropping that's even less expensive. This is something called the Spy Ear and while it's not a bug like the other devices we've been examining, it's certainly a useful addition to any spy kit. Essentially it's a sound amplifier that allows you to listen to conversations right across the room at a distance where nobody would suspect you could possibly hear them. It comes in assorted colours, batteries are included and the cost is just $8.95.

If you own a cassette recorder – and many people do – you can use it to listen in on any conversation whether you're close by or not. Most modern recorders are small and even their built-in microphones are very sensitive. Invest in a long play tape, switch on and hide the recorder in the room where the conversation will take place. Select somewhere reasonably close to where you believe your targets will be – a table drawer, for example, or a vase of flowers (with any water carefully emptied).

A small external microphone will make things easier still. These tend to be more sensitive than a built-in mike and many of them are little larger than the buttons on your coat. You can stick a mike like this under a table using poster putty or chewing gum, while the actual recorder is tucked away somewhere really safe.

Once you have the device in place, you can make yourself scarce. Collect the tape and play it back at your leisure. A voice-activated cassette recorder is particularly useful for eavesdropping operations since it will switch itself on when your targets begin speaking. Some models switch off as well, after a given period of silence, which means you will pick up more conversation per tape than you would by using a conventional recorder that's simply left running.

If you don't own a recorder and can't afford to buy one (or any of the other gadgets mentioned) there are still a few ways to eavesdrop undetected, particularly if the conversation is taking place indoors.

Low-Tech Eavesdropping

Begin by checking out any central heating system. Air ducts will often carry sound a surprising distance, so that if you sit close to the grille, you can hear a lot more than people might want you to. Even when the central heating relies on water pipes you can sometimes get lucky. All sounds are actually vibrations, and piping can act as a carrier. If you put your ear to a radiator – taking great care not to burn yourself – you can sometimes hear fragments of speech picked up by a radiator in a nearby room and carried along the piping.

Finally, never forget the old glass-against-the-wall trick. The partition walls of a house are often quite thin and may not be particularly well insulated. Placing your ear against such a wall can be enough to let you hear what's being said in the room beyond. But placing a glass against the wall and your ear against the glass works even better since the glass will act as a megaphone and amplify the sound.

SURVEILLANCE

Eavesdropping and bugging are usually just parts of a wider operation known to spies as surveillance. What that means is keeping track of somebody's movements in order to gain information about their activities.

These days, surveillance is often divided into two broad categories – high-tech and low-tech.

Going High-Tech

High-tech surveillance is particularly popular in the United States where operatives use satellite cameras, directional microphones, night scopes, radar and enough computing power to launch a spaceship just to watch a target pop out for a bag of chips. The sophistication of their equipment is awesome. On a clear day, it's now possible for a satellite in orbit above the Earth to record the headline of the newspaper you're reading in your back yard.

The price of the equipment can be pretty awesome too. You can buy night vision binoculars easily enough, but they'll set you back almost $700. You don't even want to know how much it would cost you to launch a spy satellite.

All the same, you can set up your own affordable high-tech surveillance system using just your desktop PC and an Internet connection. The trick is to use webcams.

Webcams are video cameras linked to the Internet. What they're pointed at varies from ordinary people at work in their office to the current view of Sydney Harbour in Australia. Traffic cameras in many major cities feed into the Internet – don't ask me why. There are webcams in zoos, watching the animals. There are webcams recording archaeological digs. There are webcams on safari in Africa, webcams in people's houses, trained on the occupants like contestants in *Big Brother*. There are webcams on street corners, webcams at tourist attractions, webcams on ships at sea.

And once you know how, you can have any or all of those webcams at your fingertips for your next high-tech surveillance operation.

Start by pointing your browser at http://www.camcentral.com/ or http://www.earthcam.com/. Either of these websites will give you an idea of the potential. On the Earthcam site there are links to webcams in offices and restaurants, parks and schools, clubs and churches, science labs and news rooms, at sporting events, on beaches, up mountains. You can even watch what's happening to the Space Shuttle. At Webcam Central, you can entertain yourself by typing in the name of a city you'd like to visit and finding out whether there's a camera operating. Most times there is, even in the strangest places.

The result of this is that you can watch people in Times Square, New York, right now, right on your computer screen, without leaving your room. And you can do it unobserved, undetected and quite legally.

But that's not all. If you log on to http://www.icammaster.com/ you can download a free application – Windows and Mac versions both available – that links you to a thousand webcams with the ability to add more as you go. Once you find the cam you want, you can tear it off and leave it running on your desktop so you can continue your surveillance of the site while working on something else.

Although this is the sort of high-tech capability the FBI would have killed for only thirty years ago, it has its limits. There are some surveillance jobs that simply can't be done at a distance. They need

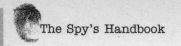

the personal touch – and that means good old-fashioned leg-work.

Going Low-Tech

For this type of low-tech surveillance, you need a particular type of person. Use the Surveillance Operative Evaluation Form below to test members of your spy ring before sending them out on a covert job.

SURVEILLANCE OPERATIVE EVALUATION

Please answer the following questions honestly and to the best of your ability. Remember, it's your head on the block if you're evaluated wrongly.

1 Are you physically fit?   ☐ *Yes* ☐ *No*

2 Do you have good eyesight?   ☐ *Yes* ☐ *No*

3 Do you have good hearing?   ☐ *Yes* ☐ *No*

4 Do you have a good memory
   for details?   ☐ *Yes* ☐ *No*

5 Are you observant?   ☐ *Yes* ☐ *No*

6 Are you extraordinarily good-looking?   ☐ *Yes* ☐ *No*

7 Would you describe
   yourself as......   ☐ *fat*   ☐ *thin*   ☐ *average?*

8 Rate your ability as an actor
   (1 = useless; 10 = brilliant)   ☐ *1* ☐ *2* ☐ *3* ☐ *4* ☐ *5*
                                                ☐ *6* ☐ *7* ☐ *8* ☐ *9* ☐ *10*

9 Are you confident about talking
   to people?   ☐ *Yes* ☐ *No*

10 Do you stand out in a crowd?   ☐ *Yes* ☐ *No*

11 Are you better as a team player or as a loner?
   ☐ *team player* ☐ *loner* ☐ *much the same at both*

12 Do you talk a lot? ☐ *Yes* ☐ *No*

13 Please rate the way you dress
   ☐ *individualistic* ☐ *height of fashion* ☐ *scruffy*
   ☐ *extremely neatly* ☐ *average*

14 Do you shave your head? ☐ *Yes* ☐ *No*

15 Is your hair dyed…
   ☐ *bright red* ☐ *green* ☐ *blue* ☐ *candy stripe*
   ☐ *natural hair colour*

16 *What is your natural hair colour?*
   ☐ *brown* ☐ *black* ☐ *fair* ☐ *white blonde* ☐ *auburn*
   ☐ *ginger*

17 How would you rate your local knowledge
   (1 = useless; 10 = brilliant)
   ☐ *1* ☐ *2* ☐ *3* ☐ *4* ☐ *5* ☐ *6* ☐ *7* ☐ *8* ☐ *9* ☐ *10*

18 How long have you been a spy?
   ☐ *less than three months* ☐ *between 3 and 6 months*
   ☐ *6 months to 1 year* ☐ *more than 1 year*

19 Do you own a comfortable pair of shoes? ☐ *Yes* ☐ *No*

20 Do you model yourself on James Bond? ☐ *Yes* ☐ *No*

EVALUATION KEY

Question   Score

1 ....Yes = 5   No = 0
2 ....Yes = 5   No = 0
3 ....Yes = 5   No = 0
4 ....Yes = 5   No = 0
5 ....Yes = 5   No = 0
6 ....Yes = 0   No = 5
7 ....Fat = 0   Thin = 0   Average = 5
8 ....Score = rating you gave yourself

9 ....Yes = 5   No = 0

10 ....Yes = 0   No = 5

11 ....team player = 5   loner = 5   both = 10

12 ....Yes = 0   No = 5

13 ....individualistic = 0 height of fashion = 0
scruffy = 0 extremely neatly = 0
average = 5

14 ....Yes = 0   No = 5

15 ....bright red = 0 green = 0 blue = 0
candy stripe = 0 natural = 5

16 ....brown = 5 black = 5 fair = 5
white blonde = 0 auburn = 5
ginger = 0

17 ....Score = rating you gave yourself

18 ....Less than 3 months = 0

between 3 and 6 months = 5

between 6 months and 1 year = 10

more than a year = 15

19 ....Yes = 5   No = 0

20 ....Yes = 0   No = 5

Rating your score

Add all the scores together, then check how the operative measures up on the table below:

Below 50   Give this operative a desk job. There's no way he or she should be sent out on surveillance work.

50 to 75   Use this operative on surveillance only if you're desperate, but don't be surprised if his/her cover is blown.

76 to 100   A good all-round surveillance operative. The higher the score the better.

100 +   An excellent surveillance operative. Use him/her when you can.

125   This is the maximum possible score and indicates that the operative cheated on the test or, alternatively, lied about the test results. Since lying and cheating are prime requisites of a spy, promote this operative at once.

SURVEILLANCE PLANNING

Once an operative is chosen, it's important to plan any surveillance operation carefully. A surveillance operation will only be as successful as the effort you put into it – and by far the most important part of that effort will be the initial preparation.

Location, Location

First, scout out the area where the surveillance will take place. Make a mental note of routes your target is likely to take and hiding places where you can watch unobserved. Plan your own escape routes should something go wrong.

Look out for the notices that will warn you if any Neighbourhood Watch Scheme is in operation. Be doubly careful if there is – the local busybodies might easily conclude you are a burglar and the last thing you need is to explain your espionage activities to the police.

Find yourself a good starting position. You need somewhere that gives you a clear view of the target and any approach routes he might use. Make sure you aren't overlooked – in other words, make sure there is no high ground or building close by that could be used by anyone to watch your activities. You should also make sure your starting position isn't somewhere that will draw attention to you.

Since a great deal of surveillance work involves nothing more exciting than just hanging about waiting for something to happen, it's a very good idea to take a packed lunch (or at least a snack) and find yourself somewhere you can eat it without drawing attention to yourself. It's also a very, very, good idea to discover the nearest loo.

Dress Code

Once you have an idea what sort of environment you'll be working in, dress yourself to suit it. In the cartoons, spies dress in trench coats with collars turned up and hats pulled well down over their eyes. But a real spy wouldn't last five minutes in that gear. What you need is something that will blend in: and that's where your knowledge of the neighbourhood becomes handy. It's no good putting on your best suit in a broken down, slum district – you'll stand out like a sore thumb. Equally, torn jeans, sneakers, skateboard and a filthy T-shirt (which would be fine in the run down district) are guaranteed to get you noticed if you're staking out a posh hotel. When you make your initial recce, take careful note of what sort of clothes the people of the district tend to wear and dress yourself to blend in. Remember, what a spy on surveillance really wants is to become the invisible man.

If you're using any special equipment, like a camera or a cassette recorder, keep it out of sight. The same goes for any papers, photographs or files you might be carrying. Those things get you noticed and may even tip off your target that he's being watched.

What's Your Story?

Decide on a cover story. There's always the possibility somebody will ask you what you're doing and you need to have a convincing explanation at the tip of your tongue. This explanation may include a whole new identity for yourself – you're a young Russian who doesn't speak much English, waiting for your aunt … you're training to join the London Philharmonic Orchestra and are on the way to your piano teacher … your poor bedridden widowed mother has sent you to the shops to buy her gin…

Whatever the story, it should be appropriate to where you are and how you look. It should sound truthful and be told without hesitation. Rehearse it in advance and try to figure out what sort of questions you might be asked and how you're going to answer them.

Your Target

Collect as much information about your target as you can. Ideally you should know his name, nickname and any alias he might be using. Find out his home address and any other addresses – like a place of employment – he habitually visits. Get his phone number.

Make sure you know what he looks like. Sounds obvious, but you'd be surprised how many surveillance operatives set out on the basis of a vague description. If you've never seen the target before, a photograph is invaluable. Failing that, never work without a detailed description covering his hair and skin colour, distinguishing features, age, height, build and the way he normally dresses.

You can pick up most of the background information you need by using the electoral register, trade directories and on-line computer searches. Asking around in his neighbourhood will produce results as well, although you have to be careful not to arouse suspicions. A good way of finding out what he looks like is to dream up some excuse for calling at his house – you might, for example, pretend to be looking for some other resident of the street. Once he opens the door you've no more worries.

With your basic survey complete and your target identified, you can decide whether the surveillance operation can be carried out solo. In certain circumstances, just one spy can keep tabs on the target, but most operations require a team. If, for example, you're watching a building waiting for the target to come out, it's impossible for just one agent to cover front and back doors at the same time. In a solo operation, your target could be long gone through the back door however carefully you watch the front.

But whether on your own or as part of a team, good surveillance requires you to fine-tune your observation skills. Take this typical example – the preliminary work you've carried out has given you the target's home address. You arrive bright and early to begin the surveillance when a nasty thought strikes you – suppose he's not at home? Suppose he got up early, or didn't come home last night, or has gone off to Bermuda for his holidays?

You could, of course, march right up to the front door and ring the bell, but you've already made one call in order to find out what he looks like. Turning up again might well make him suspicious. So what to do? This is where your observation skills come in.

Observe well

Have a look at the house. Are there any lights on? Is there smoke rising from the chimney? Is there steam on the bathroom window or emerging from vents at the side? All these signs suggest there's somebody inside. Your target may not be responsible for these signs, of course, but since it's his house chances are that it is.

Check out the curtains. If they're closed downstairs, but open upstairs, it could mean he's out of bed and getting dressed, but hasn't yet come down for his breakfast. Make careful mental note of how the house curtains were when you started the surveillance. If they change, you know there's somebody home even if you didn't actually see it happening. Other signs to look out for are:

Milk on the doorstep. One or two bottles means he's not yet left the house, otherwise he'd have taken them in. Fourteen bottles means he's gone away and forgotten to cancel the milk. (It also means he's got a particularly dumb milkman.)

The sound of machinery from inside or around the back. Some noise sources, like central heating boilers, are on automatic time switches and don't mean a thing, but the sound of power tools or a lawn mower definitely means there's somebody at home.

The behaviour of animals. A cat waiting to be let in suggests there's somebody at home. So does a hungry dog in a kennel. A dog – who can hear a whole lot better than you can – will often bark excitedly when his master gets up in the morning. You might also take note of the behaviour of birds in any trees by the house. If they all fly off suddenly, it may mean somebody has emerged out of your line of sight.

As well as using your eyes, it's a good idea to use your ears. Can you hear house doors or car doors opening or closing? Is there any indication of a gate squeaking? Can you hear the sound of somebody moving a dustbin as they put out the rubbish? Once you start to think about it, there are many household sounds that flag the fact somebody is in residence.

But however keen your senses, there will be times when you simply can't decide whether your target has left the house or not. In such circumstances, you may need to take action to find out. One simple approach is to phone the house. (You did find out the target's phone number during your preliminary preparations, didn't you?) Clearly if somebody answers, somebody is still at home. Don't just hang up when this happens, incidentally – that sounds really suspicious. Politely explain you've dialled a wrong number and apologise for the disturbance.

A Tell-Tale

Of course you can't keep ringing targets to find out if they're at home, so you might use a little advance planning to solve the problem before it actually arises. This will involve the use of a tell-tale on each of the exit doors or gates of the target's house. A tell-tale is something that lets you know when a door has been used.

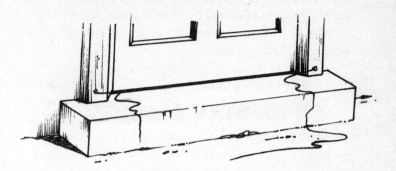

Probably the most popular tell-tale in the espionage community is a piece of thin black thread stretched between the door and its frame. Attach it near the bottom of the door and nobody will ever notice it's there, but once the door is opened, the thread breaks and a glance will tell you that your target has left.

SHADOWING A TARGET

Once your subject does leave his home, of course, you need to know how to follow him without being spotted or arousing suspicion. This process is known as shadowing and can be developed into something of an art form.

The first thing you need to realize about shadowing is that you may very well be seen. A lot of amateur spies worry about this and try to hide all the time, dodging into doorways, leaping into alleyways and generally behaving like something out of a silent movie. But the fact of the matter is there's a huge difference between being seen – which doesn't matter – and being noticed, which does.

Act Naturally

Dodging into doorways and leaping down alleyways is an excellent way of getting yourself noticed and thus should be avoided at all costs. Accept that you'll probably be seen at some stage of the operation, but ensure you won't be noticed by *acting naturally*.

If you're shadowing in a crowded street, always walk on the outside of the pavement. This makes it easier for you to see your target and cuts down on the likelihood that your view of him will be obstructed by other pedestrians at a critical moment. When the street is nearly empty, just the opposite applies. Keep to the inside of the pavement where the few other pedestrians around will provide you with a little extra cover, but are unlikely to obstruct your view.

Use the reflection of the street in various shop windows to keep an eye on your target without appearing to look in his direction. But do remember your target can look in shop windows as well and may catch too many glimpses of you. This isn't to make you paranoid, just to reinforce the earlier advice about not letting yourself be noticed.

There will be times – usually when you think everything is going swimmingly – when your target stops for no good reason, turns around and heads straight towards you. Don't panic. Chances are this *doesn't* mean you've blown your cover – it's far more likely he's just remembered he never fed the cat. What you do is act naturally, continue walking in the same direction, then casually turn the first corner you can and retrace your steps carefully until you pick up the target again.

It's generally a good idea to avoid eye contact with your target, advice that's particularly sound in the sort of situation I've just described.

From time to time your subject will turn off the street – into a supermarket or department store, for example, or into a café for a cup of tea. How you tackle these possibilities is important to the success of your mission and will vary in accordance with the circumstances.

Your first decision is whether to follow your target into the building. If the building is a small supermarket, you might consider it best to remain outside. Small supermarkets usually have only one entrance and exit. If you observe it carefully, you'll easily pick up the target when he comes out again. (There is, of course, the outside possibility that he's realized he's being shadowed and will use a back door of the supermarket to escape, but if you've been doing your job properly, it's far more likely that he's popped in for a packet of cornflakes.)

Large supermarkets and department stores usually have more than one entrance and exit. In cases of this type you have no alternative to entering the building. Don't let this worry you. You may have left the street, but during business hours you're still in a public place and as a member of the public you've every right to be there. Remember to act naturally. You might buy yourself a bar of chocolate in the supermarket or examine a piece of furniture in a department store. If salespeople approach you, simply tell them you're 'just looking'.

Remember that both supermarkets and department stores often have their own security personnel trained to look out for any suspicious characters. So if you walk in festooned with spy cameras or miniature recorders and proceed to dodge behind pillars, you may find yourself the target of some very nasty surveillance. Even if you don't notice any security personnel, you should remember virtually every major store now uses closed circuit TV to keep an eye on suspicious customers. The answer, as always, is to look and act natural.

If your target enters a café, it's usually a good idea to follow. You could remain outside watching the door – most cafés have only one entrance and exit – but the target might remain inside for quite some time which increases the chances of somebody wondering why you're hanging about.

Once you're inside, sit near the target, but not necessarily facing him. (So long as you can see the door, you won't lose him when he decides to leave.) Don't order yourself a hot drink: it could look suspicious if you have to exit early and leave it half finished, whereas you can always finish up a cold drink quickly.

Things become a little more tricky – but still manageable – if your target hops on a bus or decides to take a train somewhere. Unless you're prepared to stop the surveillance, you've really no option except to pile in there with him.

In a bus, you should sit behind him in order to keep him in view unless the bus is a double decker and he goes upstairs, in which case you should sit downstairs near the back so you know at once when he leaves. (The only exception to this rule arises when you suspect your target has gone upstairs to meet someone. In that case you should go upstairs too and try to find a seat where you can overhear what's being said.)

In a train station, you should get directly behind your target at the ticket office so you can hear where he's going and buy your own ticket to the same destination. If for some reason you can't overhear, you'll have to ask the clerk for a ticket to 'the same place he's going to'. You'll note this approach really only works if you're next in line to the target.

Stand close enough to the target on the platform to keep him in sight at all times. (In case he decides not to take the train at the last minute.) Once the two of you are on the train, you can relax a little until you reach the destination – especially if it's an express train – because your target really has nowhere to go. But stick close as he disembarks, since there are so many possible ways he might go.

Two particularly tricky areas on a surveillance job are phone boxes and lifts. You need to be particularly wary if the target enters either. In a phone box, even if he's distracted by making a call, your target has a clear view on three sides and little else to do except look around him. That means his chances of spotting you increase.

(Incidentally, it's always a good idea to check out the phone box after your target has vacated it. He may have left a message behind for a contact – phone boxes are often used as dead drops – or scribbled an important number in the margin of the directory.)

Lifts can be trickier still since, unlike a phone box, you're forced to make an on-the-spot decision about whether you should get in there with him. If you're fit, it might be better to use the stairs and take up direct (if breathless) surveillance again when he emerges. The problem with entering the lift is that you get so close to the target he is almost bound to notice you following him later.

All the same, if you *do* decide to get into the lift, you can make the best of a bad situation by avoiding eye contact and taking control of the lift buttons if at all possible. If you're effectively working the lift, it's perfectly natural for you to ask him which floor he wants; and you might even find yourself engaged in casual conversation without arousing suspicion.

But once you find yourself in close confines with a target, your only hope of escaping detection by him later is to become a master of disguise.

MASTERING DISGUISE

If some interfering busybody were to ask you how you recognize a friend in the street, chances are you'd say you know his face. Which is true enough, but doesn't explain how you recognize a friend from behind or know him when he's too far away for you to see his face clearly.

You might be tempted to say that in those circumstances you know his body shape. Which is also true enough, but doesn't explain how you recognize a friend when he's wearing a bulky overcoat.

It's In The Walk

In fact, the one thing above all others you use to recognize friends is the way they walk. You may have noticed at Hallowe'en that a friend can put on a mask and change his clothes, but you'll still know who he is if he doesn't do something about his gait. Spies use this fact as their first step towards becoming Masters of Disguise. If you change your walk really effectively, you can often fool people *without doing another single thing to disguise your appearance.* Afterwards they'll say, 'I saw somebody who looked just like young Sheila today, but I don't think it could have been her.'

So how do you change your walk?

Some spies swear by 'special effects' like faking a limp. These certainly have their place and I'll tell you about some of them in a minute. But you'll find they all come with a built-in problem – you have to remember to use them. That's far more tricky than you'd think. The way you walk is such an automatic part of you that you'll find yourself dropping back into old habits the minute you get distracted. What you really need, before you start messing around with any fancy special effect, is something that will change your gait permanently, automatically, and in such a way that you never have to think about it.

That means monkeying around with your shoes.

Make yourself a couple of small wedges out of wood covered with padding so you won't find them too crippling and slip them into your shoes. Now try walking. You'll discover instantly that the way you walk has changed, because a wedge has the effect of shifting your centre of balance.

Experiment with where you place the wedges. If you set them towards the heel, your foot will be forced up and forward, a little like a girl wearing high heels. This has the effect of throwing your body backwards to compensate. Just the opposite happens if you set the wedges towards the toe. Your foot is tilted backwards and your body is thrown forwards as if you were climbing a hill. The change in body posture can be quite subtle, but that's all it needs to be.

You can fiddle with the wedges until they've helped you develop a new style of walking that you like. (You can get some interesting results if you put them in different places in each shoe.) With this new style as your bedrock, you can start to bring in one or more of the special effects.

The oldest special effect in the book is the limp. Try not to overdo it. Some spies limp as if they had a foot crushed by a herd of stampeding bulldozers, but a slight limp is far more convincing. (After all, the sort of serious injury that leads to a bad limp would have your foot in plaster.) Be sure to remember which foot is limping. There have been spies caught because they limped into a room on their right foot and limped out again on their left. If you don't trust yourself to remember – and as I mentioned before it's not easy – a simple solution (other than the wedge) is to slip a pebble into one shoe. This will help you maintain a real limp without effort.

A dramatic variation on the limp is the stiff leg special effect. This one has the added benefit of being rather fun since you can drag one leg along behind you like the monster in a horror movie. Here again you can help yourself remember by wrapping a scarf or bandage tightly around one knee. This makes it difficult to bend and thus keeps the stiff leg in place automatically. Another way to achieve the same result is to strap a short ruler to the back of your leg.

There are two simple special effects that will profoundly influence your walking posture. One is to walk with your toes pointed in, the other is to walk with your toes pointed out. Try them and see. With your toes pointed in, you'll find you tend to take shorter steps and throw your body a little forward. Point them out and you'll tend to stomp around flat-footedly. (The effect is increased if you bend your knees slightly.)

If you wear shoes a couple of sizes too big for you, this will enable you to shuffle consistently, another useful special effect. Add to the impact by leaning forward with your head down.

Other simple, but extremely useful, effects related to your style of walking include speeding up and striding. These sound much the same, but aren't. Speeding up is just what it says on the tin – increasing the rate at which you place one foot before the other. You don't have to lengthen your stride or anything of that nature, but it will help if you keep your head high and lean slightly backwards. One authority recommends keeping your hands behind your back like Prince Charles.

Striding often involves quickening your pace, but that isn't the actual point of the exercise. March along taking giant steps, placing your heels down first and swinging your arms briskly. You'll look different – which is the aim of all these special effects – however quickly or slowly you move.

Most funny walks attract far too much attention to be useful in espionage work, but there is one interesting exception for female spies – the pogo walk. To develop the pogo walk, you need to wear high heels, take tiny mincing steps and bounce on each. The result looks odd, but strangely natural and if you're confident you'll get away with it.

Finally, there are two body postures that can be combined with a variety of walks to create a different special effect each time. The first is the slouch, something I have practised successfully since childhood. Hands in pockets, hunch forward and off you go. The second is the backstab. Bend back and to one side, as if you had lumbago and off you go again.

Once you've fixed your walk, you can go on to disguising the next most important bit of yourself. Which isn't your face, whatever you might believe, but your body.

Changing Your Body Shape

This makes sense as well once you start to think about it. Your body is many times larger than your face (unless you're a very odd looking individual, in which case you have no business being a spy) and so will make much more of a visual impact, especially at a distance.

Changing the shape of your body is easy, but the change can only run one way. If you're small and/or thin, you can easily get bigger, but short of surgery you can't really get smaller if you're big. You can, however, get bigger still, which cuts the mustard nicely since the only thing you're after is a change in your appearance.

You can play about with your height by playing about with your shoes. When I was a teenager I worried that I'd never make the basketball team, I used to pore over advertisements for *Yankee Lifters*, a pair of patent devices you slipped into your shoes to achieve a comfortable height increase. If they're still on the market, you might usefully buy yourself a pair, but if not, then the sort of wedges mentioned in the walks section will have the side-effect of a noticeable height change.

Wedges aren't the most comfortable footwear in the world, so if it's only height you want without a change of walk, you may be better off building up your shoes using insoles cut from paper or card. This will give you some height increase, but not a lot. A simpler solution, if you have the cash for it, is to buy yourself a pair of ultra thick-soled shoes and wear them only when you're on spying duty. If you're a girl, you can go the whole hog and invest in high heels (but remember they're murder to walk in during a long spell of surveillance). You might also put your hair up, which creates an illusion of extra height.

Increasing your bulk is simplicity itself, although you're going to need larger clothes than you usually wear. Your nearest charity shop could be worth a call – it will usually have great second-hand gear at a fraction of the usual cost. Collect a few old scarves, towels and cushions to use as padding. Equip yourself with a generous quantity of nylon string. (It doesn't *have* to be nylon, but it does have to be strong. Nothing will blow your cover faster than a stomach that keeps slipping down around your knees because the string has broken.)

Don't overdo the changes. You're not trying to turn yourself into the Michelin Man, just introduce enough differences to make you look like somebody you're not. For example, a towel slung across your shoulders, underneath a large jacket, will make them look broader and more muscular. You can bulk out your legs or arms, by wrapping them with scarves. A well-placed – and well-tied – cushion

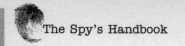

will give you the sort of beer-belly that would be a total disgrace at your age. It will also give you a very impressive behind.

In each case, make the changes on top of your normal clothes, then cover them up with a second layer of outer clothing large enough to accommodate them comfortably.

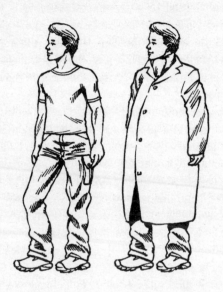

Shape and walk changes can go a long way towards making you a Master of Disguise, but you'll have to go further for close-up work. But before you reach for the false beard, there's something you should know. An analysis of police reports confirms that most witnesses really only notice one or two dominant features in the criminal who robs them. Although (hopefully) you aren't planning to rob many people, this is something you can put to good use when you're planning a disguise.

Be Dramatic

What it comes down to is you don't always have to modify your whole appearance. You simply have to make one really dramatic change that will attract everybody's attention.

Obviously this won't be enough for prolonged close contact with a target, but it's extremely useful as a way of diverting attention during a brief, casual meeting.

For example, if you put one arm in a sling, you stop being yourself and become 'some kid with a broken arm'. You can make yourself a sling easily enough using a scarf or square of material. Fold it in half to make the cradle and ask a friend to tie the ends behind your neck. But make sure he ties them loosely. This isn't a real sling, so it doesn't have to support the weight of a plaster cast – it's a disguise feature that you'll want to remove and put away quickly when the need arises.

Another easily arranged dramatic feature is a bandaged head. Take time to make it look professional (i.e. neat) and you kill two birds with one stone: you become 'some kid with a head wound' while at the same time hiding the colour of your hair.

Years ago, an advertising agency used a model with an eye patch to promote Hathaway shirts. The campaign was extraordinarily successful and the model became very well known…but only so long as he wore his patch. He told a magazine journalist that once he took it off, people failed to recognize him.

You can become the spy with the eye patch for no more effort than it takes to cut one out from black cardboard and thread it through with a length of elastic.

If you're prepared to put up with flak from your parents and friends, you can change your appearance quite dramatically by blacking out a few of your teeth. Boot polish tastes vile (I tried it once) and paint is a little too permanent, as well as often being toxic, but you can usually find something suitable in a joke shop or theatrical costumier. While you're in the joke shop, have a look at any of the sets of false teeth you can afford. Nothing will change the overall appearance of your face as effectively as a set of realistic novelty teeth.

Finally, you can give yourself a convincing war wound – and become the 'kid with the hideous cut' – by using transparent rubberized glue. Spread a little over an area of skin, then pinch it

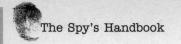

into a ridge as it begins to dry. Embed short lengths of black thread into the glue at right angles to the ridge to look like stitches. When the glue is completely dry, paint a blood red line along the length of the ridge. Properly positioned, this ghastly little experiment will make you look like something from the *Curse of Frankenstein*.

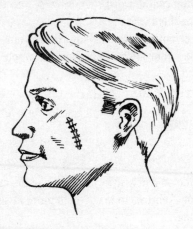

Combined with a nice black eye, a few facial cuts like the one you've created above will transform you into 'the kid whose parents beat him up'. You can fake a black eye painlessly by brushing some of your mother's blue eye shadow around it, then using your finger to smudge it in.

Using Cosmetics

Cosmetics generally can go a long way towards changing the way you look, especially if you don't get too close to a target. Since your mother won't thank you for stealing hers all the time, you might think of buying a cheap set of your own. If you do, make sure they're the type you can easily remove.

The big secret to disguising yourself using cosmetics is subtlety. And that means using as little of the cosmetics as possible to produce the desired effect. If you use a lot, you just get yourself noticed, particularly if you're a boy.

You can do a lot just by changing the appearance of your eyes. Once the eyes change, the whole face looks different.

Deft use of an eyebrow pencil will give you bags beneath your eyes while emphasizing the lines at the sides of your eyes – screw your face up to find where they are – will make you look older. Drawing on new eyebrows can be worthwhile as well. You can hide your old ones by rubbing them with thick soap.

There are, of course, ways of improving your disguise without additional make-up or getting silly about the whole thing.

Disguising Your Hair

Your hair, for example, is a very distinctive feature. Change the style – or better yet the colour – and you change your appearance. Remember to match in your eyebrows if you do change the colour – you can usually do this using an eyebrow pencil. If, on the other hand, you decide on a new style, save some of the clippings and glue them on to your eyebrows to make them more bushy. The effect can be quite amazing.

But disguise isn't all about appearance. Changing your voice can mask your identity, as can changing the way you laugh – a distinctive feature for most people. Even a new way of sneezing can help.

Change Your Habits

Don't forget to change your habits. Wear a hat if you don't normally, leave it at home if you do. Same thing goes for spectacles. Become aware of your mannerisms, the way you wave your hands around,

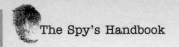

scratch your bottom or fiddle with your hair. Once you know what your mannerisms are, change them – the old familiar ways can be a dead giveaway for a spy.

PSYCHIC SURVEILLANCE

Even the best disguises can be penetrated, so there's always a chance your cover will be blown while you're collecting information. Unless, that is, you train yourself to undertake a form of spying so spooky that most people don't know it actually exists...

During the Cold War, rumours began to circulate that the Russians were using psychics to do their spying for them. Nobody believed it... except, of course, the CIA, which set up a highly secret programme of its own. The programme was called Stargate and it allowed espionage operatives to collect information from any country in the world with no risk of detection whatsoever.

All this came to light when former operatives like Major David A. Morehouse and civilian recruit Inigo Swann published books detailing their experiences. The information they gave made it clear that Stargate methods involved training in sensing things at a distance. An elite corps of CIA operatives undertook bizarre mind-journeys to target sites and brought back accurate information about what they found there.

It also became clear that while there were certain operatives who were extremely good at mind-journeys, almost anyone could get some positive results if they were prepared to put in enough time and effort.

Psychic spying allows you to get into areas so well guarded it would be dangerous to try any other way, to find out what your enemies are planning with no chance of their ever finding out you've spied on them and, above all, to collect information at no risk to yourself whatsoever.

You can find out whether you have the makings of a psychic spy by following this simple, three-step training programme.

Step One: Relaxing

Deep relaxation – the sort you need before you can go mind-travelling – takes a little practice. Find yourself a comfortable chair (don't lie on a bed since you'll only fall asleep) and spend a few minutes on the following sequence:

Tighten your arms rigidly - hold, then sigh and relax them.

Think about your chest. Tighten the muscles, hold it, sigh, then relax them.

Now concentrate on your back. Tighten the muscles, then relax them with a sigh.

Turn your attention to your hands. Curl them into fists, hold the tension, become aware of the way your fingernails dig into your palms, keep your hands tense a little longer then sigh and let them relax.

Think about your thigh muscles. Tighten, hold, sigh and relax them.

Next think about your calf muscles. Tighten them as before, hold the tension, think about the tension, then sigh, let go and relax them.

Think about your feet. Wiggle them. Curl your toes downwards to tense the muscles, then sigh aloud, let go and allow everything to relax.

Bring your attention to your scalp. Frown to tighten the scalp muscles, feel the way your scalp moves, hold everything tight for a moment, then sigh aloud and let go.

Concentrate on your face. Grit your teeth and contort your features to tense up the facial muscles then sigh and relax them.

Follow exactly the same procedure with your neck. Tighten the muscles then relax them.

Bring your mind to your shoulders, another very common tension focus. Hunch your shoulders to tighten the muscles, hold the tension, then sigh aloud as you relax them.

Concentrate on your stomach muscles, a very common tension focus.

Think about your buttock muscles. Tighten your bottom, then sigh and relax.

By this point you should be feeling pretty relaxed, but you can get more relaxed still. Close your eyes and imagine your whole body getting heavier and heavier, as if it were turning to lead. You'll find this increases your level of relaxation still further.

Now tighten up every muscle in your body, holding your entire body momentarily rigid, then relax, letting go as completely as you can. Do this final whole-body sequence three times in all. On the third time, take a really deep breath when you tense the muscles and sigh deeply aloud as you let the tension go.

That completes Step One of your mind-travel programme. Run through this sequence every morning and evening for at least two weeks before moving on to Step Two.

Step Two: Training

Once you've learned how to relax completely, you can begin your psychic espionage training by finding a comfortable chair in a room where you won't be disturbed. Leave aside twenty minutes to half an hour each morning for your session. Begin by relaxing completely, exactly as you did in Step One.

Now imagine you're no longer in your chair, but standing about 2 metres away. Try to visualise yourself as clearly as you can. Make a real effort to see the detail in your mind's eye. Imagine the scuff marks on your shoes. Count the buttons on your coat. Note the way your hair falls over one eye. Examine the expression on your face.

Spend as much time as you need to build up this imaginary figure fully. A good idea is to set aside a particular time each day for the exercise and devote ten to fifteen minutes daily to it for two weeks or more. Above all, don't rush it.

If you do this, you'll find the whole thing becomes easier until the time comes when you can sit down, relax and see yourself in all your gory detail with no effort whatsoever. When that day comes, you can go on to the next part of your training.

Take a look around the room and try to remember all the details. Now close your eyes and visualise it. If you find that difficult, open your eyes again and take another look. Keep working at it until you can describe the room in detail with your eyes closed.

When you've done that, imagine yourself rising from your chair and walking slowly round the edges of the room in a clockwise direction. Try to see in your mind's eye how the perspective of the room changes as you move. Try to remember those small objects and ornaments you couldn't see from your chair. Visualise one.

If you have problems with this part of the exercise, open your eyes, stand up *physically* and walk clockwise around the room. Then sit down, close your eyes again, and try to duplicate the journey in your imagination. Keep working on it until your visualisation becomes easy and clear.

Now try the same walk *anti-clockwise*.

After a while you'll find the whole thing doesn't take much effort any more. When this happens, try visualising yourself in another room. Pick one you know well and again walk around it clockwise, then anti-clockwise in your imagination.

You'll probably find your mental pictures are coming more easily now because of all the practice – it's a bit like working out: your muscles protest a bit at first, but after a while it all goes much more smoothly. When you've explored the second room thoroughly, visualise yourself wandering throughout your whole house.

If you have problems visualising, just keep trying. There's no time limit and, as everybody tells you, practice makes perfect. Even if you only devote ten minutes a day to the exercise, you'll get there eventually so long as you stick at it and practise regularly.

The final step in your training is to imagine yourself exploring some distant, less familiar scene. Indoors is easier to most people, but if you are feeling really confident, you might try imagining yourself in an outdoor location. Once again, you should try to examine your surroundings in as much detail as possible. Continue with this part of the exercise until it becomes easy for you.

Step Three: Testing

You're now ready to find out whether your training has given you the real ability to mind travel. The CIA often 'sent off' their operatives using a large-scale map of the target location. You can do the same.

Get hold of an Ordnance Survey map of a district near you, but make sure it's an area you haven't visited and don't know through photographs or any other means. Spread the map out on the table and pick a target location. Mark it lightly in pencil with an **X**.

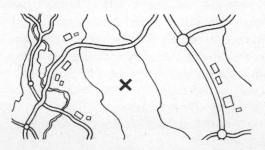

Spend a little time examining the map and noting its major features. Now get back into your comfy chair, close your eyes and try to picture the map in your mind. As always, if you find you can't quite manage it, open your eyes and take another look. Do this as often as you need – you're trying to discover if you have an interesting ability, not pass an exam.

Once you can picture the map reasonably well, imagine yourself drifting above it and – this is the trick – looking down on it *as if it was the actual landscape it depicts*. In other words, imagine yourself flying above the area shown in the map. Relax into this. It's fine to think of yourself as an eagle or some other soaring bird. It's fine to have fun and explore, enjoying the sensations of imaginary flight.

After you've been flying around for a while, head for your target location. When you reach it, swoop down and make a careful mental note of what's down there. If you find a building, try to remember exactly what it looks like, how many windows it has, what colour the front door is painted and so on. If there are no buildings, look out for natural landmarks, roads, streams, large trees or whatever. Make a real effort to remember in detail what you see.

When you've done this, return to your chair and open your eyes. Now write down everything you saw at your target location. This is very important. Experience shows that you'll quickly forget the details of any information you pick up in this way, much the same as you've now forgotten the dreams you had last night. So write down everything as soon as you open your eyes.

Now you come to the crunch. Get out your bike and go and visit the actual target location. Compare what's there with what you 'saw' in your imagination. Don't expect the picture you had in your mind to be perfect, especially the first few times you try this, but look instead for any items on the ground that coincide with your vision. They might be in a slightly different place or perhaps show a different colouring. But the important thing is that they're really there.

If you find more than one or two 'coincidences' between your vision and reality, then congratulate yourself... and keep practising your psychic espionage!

HIDING THE INFORMATION

Techniques like surveillance, disguise and bugging can collect a lot of information for your spy ring and it's important that you take all necessary precautions to keep it safe. A good spymaster always assumes his uncle will be discovered one day and tries to make sure his precious hoard of information isn't discovered with it.

A Security System

What you need to set up is a security system. For people who aren't spies, this means some sort of burglar alarm which basically makes a noise to scare intruders off and alert people that a break-in is in progress. But a spy thinks differently. A spy doesn't necessarily want to scare away intruders (for reasons I'll explain in a minute), but he certainly wants to know if they've intruded.

Your security system is in three parts. The first part is a complete set of *false* information papers. These should give totally incorrect information on your spy ring, complete with wrong names and fictional details of your operations. You can have a great time drawing up these papers if you use your imagination since they enable you to tell lies about absolutely anyone. Make sure to send your enemies off on a few wild goose chases by including maps of fake dead letter drops in difficult places.

It's a very good idea to use codes or ciphers in any of the apparently more sensitive papers, otherwise they'll look suspicious.

But make the codes easy to crack or, alternatively, get a little careless about leaving a key. The whole point about these papers is that any enemy who finds them will be sent off on completely the wrong track and, more importantly, won't bother to continue looking for any genuine information you might be hiding.

Put the papers away somewhere. The hiding place should not be too obvious, but at the same time somewhere certain to be discovered if the place is thoroughly searched – underneath your shirts in a drawer, for example, or tucked away at the back of the top shelf of a cupboard. You want them to be found, but you also want your enemies to believe you made an attempt to conceal them.

The second part of your security system involves making some hiding places that won't be found, however thorough the search. In each case the basic principle is camouflage – the hiding place has to look like something it isn't. Here are three possibilities. By the time you've made them, you should be able to think of a few more for yourself.

1. The Secret Book Store

This is an oldie but goodie, especially if you have several shelves of books in your uncle.

Slip off to your nearest car boot sale or second-hand book shop and buy yourself a copy of the cheapest old book you can find. Try to find one with a title that's dull and unappealing – something on goat husbandry or advanced mathematics would be ideal – but make sure it's at least 250 to 300 pages long, otherwise it'll be too thin to be of use to you.

Take the book home and open it up to around page 10. To turn your book into a secret book store, you're going to need a metal ruler, a sharp knife or scalpel (take care), glue and a lot of patience.

Using the ruler as a guide, carefully cut out the complete type area of the right hand page, leaving the margins intact.

Do the same to the page below, and the page below that. When you get the hang of it, you can start cutting out several pages at once. But stop about ten pages short of the end of the book and at all times make sure you don't damage the covers.

When you've finished, you'll have something that looks like an ordinary book when it's closed, but shows a hollow middle when you open it. You may also find that once you do so, the mutilated pages in the middle flap about all over the place or even tear, but don't worry about it because this is where your glue comes in. Your next step is to glue the margins together neatly so that when the glue dries you're left with what is effectively a box cunningly disguised to look like a boring old book – in other words, your Secret Book Store. Papers or any small objects you want to hide can be placed inside the gimmicked book and the book itself placed on a shelf among other books.

2. The Cunning Liner

Once you understand the basic principle of the cunning liner, you can use it on files, books and even boxes to give you a secret hiding place suitable for papers, notes, lists and things of that sort.

Let's imagine you're going to put a cunning liner on to a large hardbacked notebook. Here's how you'd do it.

First cut a piece of sturdy paper to the exact size of the inside cover of your notebook. Now tape this paper to the inside cover like a liner, but tape only three sides. Although it doesn't show, what you've done here is make a secret pocket on the inside of the cover of your notebook. If you use it only for storing papers and keep the papers themselves to a minimum so there are no obvious bulges, there's no reason to suppose anything hidden here is likely to be discovered.

The same sort of cunning liner can be used on the lid of a box file, on one or more covers of a folder or anywhere else that lends itself to a hidden pocket of this type. You can make the pocket even more

secret by gluing on the liner rather
than taping it, but be sure to
use only a thin line of glue
along each of the three
edges.

3. The Secret Bottle

The secret here isn't the bottle
itself, which can be in plain view,
but the fact that the bottle isn't what it
seems to be.

You can make the simplest form of the secret bottle by getting hold
of an empty 1-or-2 litre plastic soft drinks bottle. It needs to be darkly
coloured, but many of them are these days. A big Coca-Cola bottle
is ideal.

- Using a very sharp knife, cut the bottom
  off (ask for adult help). Make your cut
  about 1 cm up from the bottom so you're
  left with a shallow dish-shaped thing that
  used to be the bottom and the rest of the
  bottle now rendered completely useless
  for the purpose for which it was made.
  However, you've got a new purpose for it,
  so don't lose any sleep.

- Fill the bottle with whatever documents
  or small items of equipment you want to
  hide, then carefully tape the bottom back
  on again using a transparent sticky tape.
  If you stand this bottle in amongst your
  other drinks bottles, you can be sure
  no-one will notice it's been gimmicked
  and your secrets will be safe until you
  need them.

A more complicated, but even more secure, form of secret bottle is the fake paint tube. This one takes a lot more effort, but the end result is worth it.

- Start off with an old empty plastic washing-up liquid bottle. Cut off the bottom as before, then cut around the top just below the sloping neck, but this time don't cut all the way – leave about 2 cm uncut to act as a hinge. Throw away the bottom you've cut off: you won't need it for this version of the secret bottle.

- Now squeeze the bottom of the bottle flat, then use any strong tape to tape it firmly into position. Take any suitably sized top from a plastic bottle and glue it on to the top of your gimmicked washing-up liquid bottle. You won't be able to screw or unscrew this new lid, of course, it's only for show anyway.

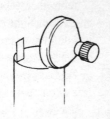

- What you now have is something that looks like a large plastic tube with a hinged top. Take a strip of thin card about 3 cm wide and glue it to the inside of the tube at the top. Make sure it sticks up a little over the edge. When the glue dries, you'll find this allows you to close the hinged top so it stays closed.

- Use acrylics or poster paints to disguise the whole thing as a paint tube. Paint the entire tube, including the collar, a single primary colour like green or red. Paint the sloping part of the collar silver so it looks like metal. You now have what looks like a large tube of paint ... all ready to keep your secrets safe from prying eyes.

The third part of your security system involves finding out whether anybody has come in to search the room where you've been hiding things. Here the point isn't to keep people out – which you'll never manage anyway if they're really determined to get in – but simply to discover if they've been, while at the same time making sure they don't discover you've discovered if they've been.

One simple but effective method is the old hairy door and windows trick, a variation of which you've already met elsewhere in this handbook. You'll need one human hair – for each door and window you want to protect. Use a dab of glue, or better yet poster putty, to fix the hair across the door or window opening.

Because it's so thin, nobody will notice a human hair unless they're looking for it. But if the door or window is opened, the hair will be broken or displaced. Either way, you will know somebody has been in while you were away.

If you'd prefer something a little more sophisticated, you can set up a marvellous security system using a set of six table-tennis balls and half a dozen cardboard tubes. You can make up the tubes yourself simply by rolling and gluing cardboard. Each one should be about 7.5 cm long and 2.5 cm in diameter.

Paint each tube a different colour – red, orange, yellow, blue, green, violet, for example, but any colours that appeal to you will do, just so long as they're all different. Now paint each table-tennis ball a different colour as well. These can be the same colours as the tubes or completely different. Here again the only really important thing is that all six balls are different from each other.

Once you've done that, your security system is ready. To use it, set the six tubes upright in a row just inside the door you want to protect. Make a note of the order of the colours from left to right. Now set a table tennis ball on top of each tube. Once again make a note of the order of the colours from left to right. You do not have to match the colour of the ball to the colour of the tube. In fact it would certainly be best if you did not match the colours in every case, although one or two matches would be absolutely fine.

What you now have is a set of six tubes with six balls balanced on top of them. Only you know the order in which the tubes are laid out and which ball goes with what tube. If anybody opens the door in your absence, tubes and balls will all go flying. And here's the sneaky bit: even if the intruder notices your security system and tries to put it together again, the chances of his figuring out the correct order of balls and tubes are hundreds to one against.

That's the basic principle of the security system, but it does have one drawback as it stands. Somebody seeing the coloured balls and tubes might suspect what you're using them for. If this worries you – and as a trained spy it should – then decorate the items to look like toys or ornaments. You might, for example, paint a smiley face on each ball and turn the tubes into stylized bodies so they become little men and women.

Once your three-pronged security system is in place, you can start to feel your spy ring is really secure.

Except, perhaps, for one little thing ...

ARE THEY WATCHING YOU?

Of course they're watching you! Every large store you walk into – and quite a few of the small ones – is equipped with CCTV, Closed Circuit Television. The Government has spent a great deal of public money to install more CCTV cameras on the streets of every major city as a way of fighting crime. Then there are those traffic cameras I mentioned earlier. And the webcams set up in public places...

Many CCTV systems have a security guard on the other end, sleepily scanning his screens to spot anything suspicious. Many more are attached to a video recorder and the tapes stored for weeks, months or even years, so there's lasting evidence of what you were doing when you walked past the camera.

All these cameras are perfectly legal, but there are unscrupulous website operators who make a career of installing illegal – and very well hidden – cameras in loos and changing rooms so they can charge people up to $19 an hour to look at your bottom. No accounting for taste, but it does happen and when the cameras are found, the operator simply writes off his loss as a business expense and installs some more.

But that's not all. Satellite systems designed to spot troop movements or similar hostile actions in enemy countries have now reached such a degree of sophistication that they can read the note you passed to your friend in the park the other day. It won't really do you much good slipping indoors either. Infra-red and radar are just two of the technologies that allow the spymasters to penetrate most buildings well enough to track everyone inside.

You'd better keep your mouth shut as well. In the bad old days of the Cold War, the Stasi (Secret Police) bugged every single phone in East Germany and employed more than 10,000 operatives to listen in to conversations. If you think that couldn't happen here, think again.

New digital ISDN systems are gradually replacing the older analogue phone lines throughout the country. They give you clearer reception for voice communications and faster log-on speeds when you're connecting to the Internet. I have one myself. The sticker on the box beside me tells me ISDN is *A New Way of Doing Business*. What it doesn't tell me (nor did any salesperson or engineer when I inquired about ISDN) is that the new digital system allows an operator at the exchange to take control of the microphone, effectively turning the unit into a bug that will pick up any conversation I have in my study.

Even if you haven't got ISDN, I wouldn't get too smug if I were you. As long ago as 1997, the Civil Liberties Commission of the European Parliament published a report confirming that every phone call, fax message and e-mail sent anywhere in Europe (including the British Isles) is routinely monitored. Nowadays you don't need the massive manpower hired by the Stasi. Electronic communications of any sort are filtered through computer systems programmed to watch out for certain keywords and switch on the recorders when they hear them.

Who's Listening In?

Well, just about the whole English-speaking world by the sound of it. What's grown into a massive electronic surveillance operation was first established back in 1947 when America, Britain, Canada, Australia and New Zealand signed a pact to continue pooling intelligence information as they'd done during World War II. Some experts are convinced the system is now capable of monitoring phone calls and reading private e-mails anywhere in the world.

Special Appendix

MAKE YOUR OWN SPY KIT

Every good spy has his or her own spy kit, the collection of special equipment that's used for certain jobs. A professional spy will typically spend hundreds, perhaps thousands of pounds on his kit, but if you're prepared to do some work, you can cut this investment down to nearly nothing.

Here are some projects that will leave you the proud owner of a first-class spy kit.

1. Identity Cards

You're on a delicate mission in dangerous territory. Suddenly a heavy hand falls on your shoulder. "What do you think you're doing snooping around Buckingham Palace at this time of night?" demands a voice that belongs to somebody a lot bigger than you are.

The hand means you can't run; and besides he's seen your face. Fortunately, having read this handbook, you have a convincing cover story ready. But when you've finished he only sniffs suspiciously and growls, "Prove it!"

One way to 'prove it' is to produce an official-looking ID card that matches the story you've just told the guard. Where can you get an ID card of that sort? You make it yourself, of course — I said official-looking, not official.

You'll need...

A small sheet of thin, plain card. White is good, but you can use yellow or pale blue as well.

- **A little red paint**
- **Glue**
- **A marker pen (black)**
- **A pencil**
- **A head-and-shoulders photograph of yourself**
- **Scissors**
- **Ruler**
- **A slice of plain white bread (No, honestly)**

- Cut a rectangle about the size of a credit card from your sheet of thin card. Round off the corners.

- Trim your head-and-shoulders picture until it's the size of a passport photo. If the job you are on calls for disguise, make sure the photo you are using shows you in the same disguise otherwise you'll defeat the whole object of the ID card.

- Place the photo in the top right-hand corner of the card and lightly draw around the four corners with your pencil to mark its position. Now carefully glue the picture in place.

- Wait until the glue has completely dried before going on to the next stage.

- Using the pencil, draw four guide-lines across the face of the card an equal distance apart. The first three will obviously end before they reach the left-hand edge of your photograph, but since the fourth is likely to be below the picture, it can continue further. Start the first one far enough down to leave room for the Issuing Organization name, something we'll get back to in a minute.

- On the left-hand side of the card at the beginning of the first line, carefully write the word 'Name', Do the same at the beginning of the second line with the words 'Birth Date', at the beginning of the

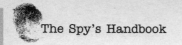

third with 'Membership Expires' and finally at the beginning of the fourth line with the word 'Signed'.

- Using your marker pen, emphasize the pencilled guide-lines by dotting them at intervals. When the ink dries, rub out the pencil marks leaving four clearly defined dotted lines. Underneath the fourth – the one that starts with 'Signature' – write the word 'Chairman' towards the right of the card.

- If you need your card to pass close scrutiny, then print the entire layout in Times Roman or some other official-looking type face using your computer, then cut it out and glue it in place. (Take care to glue it flat. There should be absolutely no bubbles or wrinkles. Indeed, if you have a computer and printer that will handle it, you should print direct on to the card.)

- At the top of the card write the name of the issuing organization. Now this is where things get interesting. You'll need to tailor the issuing organization to the cover story you'll be using, which almost certainly means you should make a series of ID cards with a different issuing organization name on each. For example, if your cover story is that you're scouting out the area for a new airfield, your ID card might be headed British Aviation Authority. If you're trying to convince people you have a right to sneak round your local mall, you might select Association of Retail Traders. Here are a few suggestions for the ID cards:

> *Aardvark Fan Club*
> *Associated Associates*
> *Associated Rhubarb Mills*
> *Brindle Cat League*
> *Campaign for Political Correctness*
> *Chocolate Prune Association*
> *Croydon Old People's Home*
> *Federated Plum Export Board*
> *International League of Wholesalers*
> *International Tree Protection Association*

London Benefit Association
Ministry of Hardship
Mole Mines
Nîmes Observatory
Official Book League
Standards Authority
U.F.O. Investigator
United Aviaries
Wall Builders Anonymous

- To complete your card, fill in your name (real or assumed according to your cover story) on the first line, a reasonable birth date on the second line, and an expiry date several months in the future on the third line. You can leave this blank until shortly before you go out on your mission since the expiry date limits the use of your card.

- Now, forge the chairman's signature on the fourth line. Pick any name you like and don't be afraid to scrawl it illegibly. Complete the card by stamping it with the official seal. This is where your slice of bread comes in. Tear off a piece and roll it into a cylinder about 1 cm in diameter. Dip the end into your red paint and use it to stamp the bottom right-hand corner of the card. You'll be astonished how official the result will look.

- If you want to give the card a really professional finish, laminate it using a small piece of transparent film.

Aardvark Fan Club

Name: ....

Date of Birth: ..../...../.....

Membership Exp: ..../...../.....

Signed: ....

CHAIRMAN

2. Spy's Newspaper

You're on surveillance and are worried that the target may have spotted you. What you need is a way to watch him without his seeing you – or at least without his knowing who you are.

One way to do it is to equip yourself with a special spy's newspaper. You can make it in a moment. Here's how...

- Take an ordinary broadsheet newspaper and set the front-page/back-page spread to one side for the moment.

- Cut two peep-holes in the remainder of the newspaper at a level that allows you to see through easily when you hold the paper up in a natural reading position.

- Now take the front-page/back-page spread and cut two peep-holes in that as well, but position them just above the peep-holes in the rest of the newspaper. This means that when you put the whole paper together again, all the peep-holes disappear. But now all you have to do is slide the front page down a little (so the holes there coincide with the rest of the paper) and you have a clear but sneaky view of your target.

3. Seebackulator

In order to maintain your cover, you've had to move ahead of your target, but you still want to keep an eye on him. There must be some way you can manage it without attracting too much attention to yourself. And there is! Here's how to make a seebackulator, a nifty piece of spy equipment that gives you eyes in the back of your head.

You'll need...
- Two small plain mirrors (the sort girls carry in their handbags are ideal)
- An old book or diary you no longer need
- Some strong adhesive tape
- Glue

- Put the two mirrors with their reflecting surfaces facing each other and tape them together at one side, so you're left with a mirror hinge.

- Take the cover and a few inside pages from the old book and glue them around your hinged mirrors. What you have now is a pair of hinged mirrors cunningly disguised as an old book.

- Carry the book with you wherever you go – nobody will pay it any attention. When you want to see what's going on behind you, simply open the book as if you were reading it and use the mirrors like the rear-view mirror of a car.

4. Spy's Shades

Spy's shades are a simple but sophisticated version of the seebackulator. To make them, you'll need a pair of large-frame sun glasses that are actually a bit too big for you and one, or possibly two, small pieces of mirror.

- Glue the mirrors onto the inside of the frames at either side of the lenses close to the hinges. If you position them properly, they'll work like a car's wing mirrors, allowing you to see behind.

5. Spy's Overseer

The spy's overseer – a pocket periscope – is a great way to watch your target over a wall or around a corner. You can buy quite good ones fairly cheaply in many toy shops, but you can also make one quickly in an emergency.

You'll need...

- **A cardboard tube** (The cardboard tube's easier than you'd think. Lurk about in the kitchen until the roll of tinfoil is finished.)
- **Two small mirrors** • **Plasticine or poster putty**

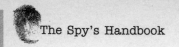

- Cut a section out of each end of the tube like this: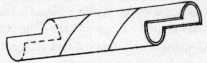

- Now use your plasticine or poster putty to fix a mirror into each end. Tilt them at an angle until you can look into one and see the view reflected in the other. You may have to fiddle around to get this right, but once you do, you've got your own spy's overseer.

6. Spy's Diary

A spy's diary is exactly like anybody else's diary – appointments, reminders, notes – except for one thing: it's entirely phony. Not one appointment, reminder, note or any other entry is genuine.

The spy's diary, as you may have guessed, is like the fake ID cards – a way of backing up a cover story. To make one, get your cover story straight then use that fine imagination of yours to create the relevant entries. Although you don't have to have an entry for every day – nobody ever does – it will still take you quite a bit of time to make up a spy's diary properly, but you'll thank yourself a thousand times when it stops your cover being blown.

You can back up the spy's diary by writing a few letters to yourself under the same assumed name. If you want to do it properly, you can post them to yourself and keep the envelope as well. The trick here is to write your address in pencil. When the letter is delivered, you then rub it out and write in a new, phony name and address in pen. The stamp will be all nicely franked with a recent date and the whole thing will look very kosher indeed.

7. Fingerprint Outfit

Fortunately you don't have to make anything this time. You just need to make sure you have a small tin of talcum powder, a roll of sticky tape and a few pieces of dark-coloured card. To collect a print, find something like a cup or a glass that you know your target has handled and dust it lightly with talcum powder. (If your hand slips,